Psychotherapeutic Reiki

Psychotherapeutic Reiki
A Holistic Body-Mind Approach to Psychotherapy

Revised and Expanded Edition

RICHARD R. CURTIN, JR., PSY.D., RMT

©2015 Cambridge Center for Change
All rights reserved
First printing of the Revised and Expanded Edition
ISBN: 978-1517285258
ISBN: 1517285259
Book production by Keystroke Studios
16 Oliver St.
Watertown, MA 02472
www.keystrokestudios.com

Cambridge Center for Change
11 Bellis Circle
Cambridge, MA 02140
www.cambridgecenterforchange.com

In the practice of Psychotherapeutic Reiki, we meet our symptoms in the silence of presence. We see them, we feel them, and we touch into them with Reiki. We hold our symptoms in the loving embrace of consciousness, Ki, and witness their transformation.

What consciousness touches, it frees.

– Adyashanti

The Original Reiki Ideals

The secret art of inviting happiness
The miraculous medicine of all diseases
Just for today, do not anger
Do not worry and be filled with gratitude
Devote yourself to your work and be kind to people
Every morning and evening, join your hands in prayer
Pray these words to your heart
and chant these words with your mouth
Usui Reiki Treatment for the improvement of body and mind

– The founder, Mikao Usui

CONTENTS

Acknowledgements

The writing of this book would not have been possible without the interest, support and contributions made by those clients and Reiki students who worked with these approaches and have furthered my learning. I am grateful to you all.

Over the past decade, I have met with and heard from a number of therapists around the country who are pioneering this work, and I am indebted to them for their suggestions and their encouragement. I especially want to acknowledge Judy Prebluda, my colleague and partner in exploring and developing the early practice of Psychotherapeutic Reiki, and my co-author for the article "Leading with Reiki and Following with Words." I would also like to thank Linda LaFlamme, Executive Director of IARP, Elise Brenner, organizer of the annual Celebration of Reiki Conference in Boston, Uli Dettling, Dennis Dettling Kalthofer, and Matt Roselli for supporting this book and this approach.

Since the publication of the first edition of this book in 2012, I have been consulting and working with other clinicians and Reiki practitioners who are using the Psychotherapeutic Reiki approach. In this second edition, I am very pleased to include techniques described in Chapter 8 by one of these clinicians, Vanessa L. Vlahakis, M.A., RMT. Vanessa was also the editor of this edition of the book, and I would like to thank her for her invaluable assistance in organizing and editing this second edition.

I would also like to thank the members of my Psychotherapeutic Reiki supervision group for their pioneering efforts in practicing and utilizing this approach: Vanessa L. Vlahakis, Linsay Preston, Patrick Teahan and Elsa Elliott.

I would like to thank Lindsey Barlow for her help in typing up this manuscript, and Hank Bonney at Keystroke Studios, who designed our website and directed the publishing of both editions of this book.

And finally, a special thank you goes to my wife Amanda Curtin, who is my partner at the Cambridge Center for Change. She is a gifted therapist and mentor, and an inspiration to me personally and professionally. Her love and support make all things possible.

To my daughters Sarah and Roo, and my grandsons James and Jake, who light up my life every week.

Introduction

I have been a practicing psychotherapist since 1975, and until my experience with Reiki energy work, I had practiced in a traditional way. I had never had any body-work treatment, not even massage, and I had no desire to try. But in the fall of 1993, during one of our weekly therapy sessions, a client of mine talked to me about her experience of receiving Reiki for a chronic pain problem. I was intrigued by her description of how this energy work brought out and released her physical pain, so I decided to try a treatment myself, as I was having chronic abdominal pain that my doctor couldn't figure out.

During my first Reiki treatment, I drifted into a pleasant and relaxing meditative state from which I observed sensations and emotions in the body and images and thoughts in the mind. In several early sessions, I had the repetitive image of being caught in a snowstorm with the snow and wind blowing all around me as the life force energy in me slowly drained away. I later came to understand this as my body's symbolic representation of my childhood experience. As I continued treatments and we focused on my abdominal pain, I discovered that this pain was actually the sensation of held trauma energy: unreleased traumatic memory stored in the body. The Reiki eventually released the effects of this traumatic memory, and the pain disappeared.

As a psychologist, I was excited by the potential that Reiki held for psychotherapy clients and I started Reiki training. After completing the Master Level in 1996, I wanted to bring Reiki into my therapy practice. Therapists have been taught and warned not to touch their clients under any circumstances. Even giving a client a hug is frowned upon, so I didn't plan to touch clients. I planned to use Reiki by sending it to clients across the room, with their permission, during our therapy sessions. I initially used Reiki in this way with the clients who were interested and open to alternative kinds of treatment. Most of these clients experienced the meditative state that I had experienced, and most felt that the Reiki helped them more clearly focus their attention on their thoughts and emotions.

However, the overall experience seemed consistently less intense than the hands-on form of Reiki treatment that I had undergone. I had one particular client, with whom I had worked for a long time, who wanted to try a hands-on Reiki treatment to see how it differed from receiving Reiki from across the room. I felt secure in my relationship with her so I brought in a massage table and gave her a treatment. She found that the hands-on Reiki treatment was stronger, seemed to go deeper and could be more easily directed to areas of the body needing attention than the distant form of Reiki I had been sending her. She decided she wanted to continue the treatments in conjunction with talk therapy. I kept the Reiki table folded up and stored in a corner of my office so as not to draw attention to it, and each week when she came in for a session I'd bring it out, set it up and after the session put it away.

Although I had not planned to use Reiki touch-treatment with clients, it seemed that the Reiki had other ideas. Other clients began asking to try hands-on Reiki during our sessions. I began to use table work with select clients with whom I felt safe enough and guided to work in this way. I was careful about whom I chose to try this with; I have had clients with whom I am not comfortable using hands-on Reiki, and I have not done so. For example, clients lacking in sufficient ego strength, clients for whom touch is intrusive or constitutes boundary confusion or boundary violation, clients with transference problems, clients who are ungrounded, and clients prone to re-traumatization or triggering are not good candidates for hands-on Reiki treatments. (These issues will be discussed later in this book in Chapter 2, "Issues with Touch in Psychotherapeutic Reiki.") Some of these clients I refer to other Reiki practitioners so as to separate bodywork from talk therapy.

Over time, and as I became more comfortable using hands-on Reiki, I rearranged my office so that I could leave the Reiki table set up and accessible. Seeing the Reiki table when they first came in for an appointment prompted new clients to ask about its use, and this gave me an opportunity to discuss my use of Reiki in conjunction with psychotherapy.

Since 1996, I have been developing ways to use Reiki

and talk therapy together in a holistic approach to psychotherapy. This book represents this evolving effort to date. Some of the interventions I discuss are techniques that I read about or learned from other clinicians and have adapted and incorporated into my work, while others have been inspired by the Reiki energy work itself. As you use Reiki you will find that the Reiki will guide you, and interventions will emerge from the work that you and your clients are doing together.

This book is for psychotherapists and counseling bodyworkers who have completed at least the first level of Reiki training, and thus presumes a basic knowledge of and ability to use Reiki. It addresses the following issues:

- How to introduce table work to clients;

- The ethics and use of Reiki touch;

- An energy model for understanding psychological problems and symptom formation;

- Treatment techniques for exploring and releasing the negative effects of held trauma energy;

- The installation of corrective cognitive and emotional experiences;

- The use of breath work;

- Ways to help clients be present in their bodies;

- Ways to clear and vitalize the Human Energy Field; and

- How to use intention and affirmation for cognitive, emotional and behavioral change.

Throughout this book, case examples are given to highlight the issues that typically arise when combining Reiki with psychotherapy. The names used in these examples are fictitious.

Every therapeutic approach has a theory base, like the trunk of an oak tree, that seeks to explain symptom formation, and it is from this trunk that specific interventions, or branches, grow.

Chapter 1

An Energy Model for Understanding Symptom Formation

Psychotherapeutic Reiki is an approach based on Eastern energy concepts, Reiki, mindfulness and Western psychological perspectives. It is used to treat psychological, emotional and behavioral problems, unresolved trauma reactions, stress, and chronic pain. This approach focuses on the body and body-mind processes as they are occurring in the present. It is an experiential approach that stresses the use of non-judgmental awareness and acceptance of experience as it is unfolding. It involves the co-participation of the client and the therapist in the investigation and treatment of problems and symptoms.

Theory Base

Implicitly or explicitly, every therapeutic approach has a theory base that seeks to explain human development, behavior and symptom formation, and it is from this theory base that specific interventions and treatment strategies are developed. Psychotherapeutic Reiki is based largely on energy field theory, energy anatomy, and Reiki, which emerged from Buddhist spirituality.

Ki Energy

Energy field theory posits that the most basic building block underlying all life forms is a subtle energy which has different names within different cultures and different disciplines, including Ki, chi, prana, bioplasmic energy, vital energy and life force energy. Ki, in the Japanese word "Reiki," refers to this subtle energy.

Ki energy is the matrix out of which life is created and evolves. It animates, regulates, organizes and supports all forms of life, and when it is withdrawn, life ceases and we die. Ki is the energetic charge underlying thought, emotion, behavior and physiological functioning. Ki energy exists in a "sea" around us, generally referred to as the Universal Energy Field (U.E.F.). This field connects all animate and inanimate objects. From a spiritual perspective, this field is thought to be divine consciousness itself.

There are many different types of Ki energy, vibrating at different frequencies and with different properties (one source I came across identified more than 200 different types or frequencies of Ki). Reiki is one type of Ki that through its long history of use has demonstrated the ability to treat imbalances in the Human Energy Field (H.E.F.).

The Human Energy Field

Every living human form has his or her own personal

energy field called the Human Energy Field, which bears the personal signature of that individual and reflects his or her own genetic makeup and personal history. Ki energy flows in and out of the body and the H.E.F. in energetic exchange with others and with the world. Ki influences and is influenced by the nature and quality of the information that is stored in the H.E.F and the U.E.F.

It is commonly thought that the H.E.F. is organized into subfields or levels and energy centers called *chakras*, which are connected to one another by energy highways called *meridians*. The various levels of the H.E.F. interpenetrate one another and extend outward from the physical body, with each successive level vibrating at a higher frequency than the preceding ones.

Barbara Brennan (1993) delineates the layers of the H.E.F. in her book, *Light Emerging*. According to her, the physical body is the densest and central part of the H.E.F., and is the vehicle of the H.E.F and the repository of the field's history and experience. Residual experiences that are carried on other layers of the H.E.F. filter down to the body. Caroline Myss (1996) writes, "In this way, our biographies are woven into our biological systems, gradually, slowly, every day" (p. 40). Myss believes that all thoughts and experiences are encoded and stored in the body and the H.E.F.

The first H.E.F. energy layer, directly next to the physical body, is called the etheric body or etheric double. This level is an "energy twin" to the dense physical body and it reflects the physical body's state of health. According to

Brennan (1993), illness and disease can be seen clairvoyantly on this level before they manifest in the body.

The next layer out is called the emotional body. The emotional body is important in healing work, as all of the "wear and tear" and stress that accumulate from living in the world are stored in this layer. Unless this stress is released it can negatively affect the health of the physical body.

The mental body is the third level of the H.E.F. and it is thought that the mind is actually located in this field and not in the physical brain. The mental level of our field contains the egoic mind and the ego's constructions of self, other, and how the world works. It is through the egoic mind that we create our lives and constructions of reality. This level of the H.E.F. greatly affects the other levels, as the meaning we make of the experiences we have contributes to our emotional state and physical health.

According to Brennan (1993), the fourth level of the H.E.F. carries the world of our relationships and is the level at which we energetically connect to others. In *Light Emerging*, Brennan depicts in dramatic drawings energetic streamers and cords connecting individuals in relationship to one another. Emotional closeness and distance, as well as whether relationships are nurturing or toxic, affect the quality and health of the energy in this field. The negative effects created by unresolved interpersonal trauma and injury can remain in the H.E.F. and affect several different energy levels besides the fourth. For example, an interpersonal trauma leads to the development of a set of beliefs and expectations in the mental body, which in turn generates emotional distress in the emotional body that becomes stored in the physical body and may manifest behaviorally or in illness of some type.

In Brennan's (1993) model, the fifth, sixth, and seventh levels of the H.E.F. represent levels of the spiritual body (divine will, divine love, and divine mind, respectively). At the spiritual level, the ego and the experience of being a separate self dissolve. At this level, we all share the same self; as Stephen Levine (1987) says, there is only one of us here. Healing on the spiritual level occurs through divine grace, and it is on this level that we make contact with our higher selves, spirit guides and other beings, and God consciousness.

THE CHAKRA SYSTEM

The chakras and energy pathways are located on the etheric body or first level of the H.E.F. The major chakras are connected to one another by a central energy channel that runs vertically up and down the center of the human body from the base of the spine to the crown of the head. There are more than 200 major and minor chakras in the chakra system, although only seven major chakras are commonly discussed or written about. Interestingly, the standard hand positions taught in Reiki treatment coordinate with these primary chakras as well as major energy meridians to treat energy imbalance and promote healing.

In her book *Eastern Body, Western Mind*, Anodea

Judith (2004) presents an excellent exposition on the relationship between psychological functioning and the functioning of the seven major chakras. She finds that the health of the chakras is greatly affected by mental, emotional, and physical conditions and conditioning. Her ideas offer a useful guide in working with chakra imbalance in the practice of Psychotherapeutic Reiki. The following discussion on the chakras is largely taken directly from her work.

First Chakra

The *first* or *root chakra* is the vibration and frequency of red light, and is located at the base of the spine and coccygeal plexus. It controls and energizes the whole visible physical body, especially the bones, blood, muscles and tissues of the body, and the internal organs, adrenal glands and sex organs. It affects body heat, general vitality, and the growth of infants and children. The developmental tasks of the first chakra are physical growth, the development of motor skills, and the psychological development of object permanence. This chakra expresses the basic right to be here on this planet. Malfunctioning of this chakra may manifest as bone cancer, disorders of the bones and teeth, leukemia, arthritis, back problems, blood ailments, allergies, frequent illness, eating disorders, growth problems, low vitality, and issues with legs, knees, feet, and the base of the spine or buttocks.

According to Judith (2004), traumas affecting the first chakra include "birth trauma, abandonment, physical neglect, poor physical bonding with mother, malnourishment, feeding difficulties, major illness or surgery, physical abuse or violent environment, enema abuse, [and] inherited traumas" from parents (e.g., Holocaust survivors, war veterans, poverty, alcoholic family systems) (p. 53). Root chakra deficiencies include the individual's disconnection from his/her body, being noticeably underweight, having poor boundaries with others, being restless and ungrounded, suffering from fear and anxiety, struggling with financial difficulties, and being unfocused, undisciplined and disorganized. Root chakra excesses may be seen in "obesity, overeating, hoarding, material fixation, greed, fear of change, addiction to security, rigid boundaries" and being sluggish, lazy or chronically fatigued (Judith, 2004, p. 53).

Healing practices to help balance the root chakra include grounding and reconnection to the body, physical exercise, touch therapy, massage, bioenergetic grounding, Hatha yoga, psychotherapy to work on one's earliest childhood maternal relationship, and reclaiming the right to exist.

Second Chakra

The *second* or *sacral chakra* is the vibration and frequency of orange light, and is located in the lower abdomen and sacral plexus. This chakra controls and energizes the reproductive organs, spleen, urinary system and bladder. The developmental tasks of the second chakra are the sensory exploration of the world, movement, procreation, and the healthy expression of sexuality and creativity. This chakra expresses the basic rights to feel and experience pleasure. The ajna (third eye), throat, and root chakras have a strong influence on the functioning of the second chakra. Imbalance in any of these may result in malfunctioning of the second chakra.

According to Judith (2004), conditions that adversely affect the sacral chakra include "sexual abuse (covert or overt), physical and emotional abuse, volatile situations, neglect, coldness, rejection, denial of a child's feeling states, lack of mirroring, enmeshment, emotional manipulation, religious or moral severity," and living in alcoholic family systems (p. 104). These conditions may result in disorders in the above mentioned organs as well as menstrual difficulties, sexual dysfunction, lower back pain, knee difficulty, physical inflexibility, numbed senses, loss of interest in food, sex, and life, and creative blockages.

Imbalance of this chakra can also create deficiencies such as "rigidity in body and attitudes, frigidity, fear of sex, poor social skills, denial of pleasure, excessive boundaries, fear of change, [and] lack of desire, passion, and excitement" (Judith, 2004, p. 105). Sacral chakra excesses can include sexual acting out, sexual addiction or sexual manipulation, addiction to pleasure, poor personal boundaries, disregarding others' boundaries, excessively strong emotions, emotional dependency or being ruled by emotion, and obsessive attachment.

Healing practices to help balance the second chakra include dance and movement therapy, emotional release or containment work (as appropriate), "inner child work, boundary work, 12-step programs for addictions," and the development of sensory intelligence and personal responsibility for behaviors (Judith, 2004, p. 105).

Spleen, Navel and Meng Mein Chakras

Between the sacral chakra and the solar plexus chakra are three minor chakras that Choa Kuk Sui (1990) describes in his book *Pranic Healing* as essential in energy treatment: the *spleen, navel* and *Meng Mein chakras.*

The spleen chakra is located on the front left part of the abdomen between the front solar plexus chakra and the navel chakra (in the middle of the bottom left rib). The spleen chakra is another entry point for Ki energy into the body and H.E.F., and plays a major role in one's general well-being and vitality. The back spleen chakra is located in the corresponding area on the back of the body and serves the same function.

The navel chakra is located at the front near the navel. It controls and energizes the small intestine, lower large intestine, adrenal glands and appendix. It affects the general vitality of a person. The navel center produces a type of "synthetic Ki" that helps the body and H.E.F. to draw in, distribute, and assimilate Ki energy. Navel chakra deficiency may manifest as constipation, appendicitis, difficulty in giving birth, low vitality, and diseases related to the intestines.

The Meng Mein chakra is located at the back of the navel. It serves as a pumping station in the spine that is responsible for the upward flow of Ki energies coming from the first chakra. It controls and energizes the kidneys, the adrenal glands and blood pressure. Malfunctioning of the Meng Mein chakra may manifest as kidney problems, low vitality, high blood pressure, and back problems. Healing practices that help to balance these chakras are the same as practices discussed under the second and third chakras.

Third Chakra

The *third* or *solar plexus chakra* is the vibration and frequency of yellow light, and is located at the solar plexus, the hollow between the bottom of the ribs, right above the belly button. It controls and energizes the pancreas, liver, diaphragm, large intestine, appendix, and stomach. The developmental tasks of the solar plexus chakra are the establishment of an individual identity and the ability to act in a functionally autonomous manner: responsibly, reliably, balanced, able to meet challenges, and with healthy self-worth, self-esteem, good ego strength, appropriate self-discipline, confidence, and warmth in personality. This chakra expresses the basic right to act as an autonomous individual in this world.

The solar plexus chakra is quite sensitive to emotion, tension and stress and has a strong influence on the physical heart. Malfunctioning of the solar plexus chakra may cause malfunctioning in the heart. The solar plexus serves as an energy-clearing house for the body and H.E.F. (subtle energies from the lower chakras and higher chakras pass through it as a central channel).

Traumas that adversely affect this chakra come from shaming experiences, authoritarianism, volatile or dangerous situations and environments, physical abuse, fear of punishment or harm, subjugation of will, enmeshment or parentification, and emotional manipulation. These types of trauma may result in an individual having low energy, weak will, low self-esteem, poor self-discipline, victim mentality, excessive passivity and susceptibility to manipulation, poor digestion, and an attraction to sedatives.

Conversely, chakra excess may result in an individual being overly aggressive, dominating, controlling, manipulative, power-hungry and deceitful, needing to be right all the time, being prone to tantrums and angry outbursts, having driven ambition (as in Type-A personality), and being competitive, arrogant and stubborn.

Healing practices that help to balance the solar plexus chakra include "grounding and emotional contact, deep relaxation, stress control, vigorous exercise, martial arts, psychotherapy [with a focus on] building ego strength, releasing or containing anger, working on shame issues, strengthening the will, encouraging autonomy," and learning to interact in more direct and adaptive ways (Judith, 2004, p. 166).

Fourth Chakra

The *fourth* or *heart chakra* is the vibration and frequency of green light, and is located at the center of the chest. It energizes and controls the heart, the thymus gland, and the circulatory system. The back heart chakra controls and energizes the lungs, and to a lesser degree, the heart and circulatory system. The developmental task of the heart chakra is the ability to form intimate friendships and social relationships, as well as the ability to love oneself unconditionally. This chakra expresses the basic rights to love and be loved. Malfunctioning of the heart chakra may manifest in heart and circulatory illnesses, eating disorders, digestive disorders, chronic fatigue, hypoglycemia, diabetes, muscle spasms, muscular disorders, and hypertension.

According to Judith (2004), traumas and abuses affecting the heart chakra include "rejection, abandonment, loss, shaming, constant criticism, sexual or physical abuse, betrayal, divorce," loveless or emotionally cold environments, and unacknowledged and unresolved grief (p. 222). Symptoms of heart chakra deficiency may be seen in antisocial behavior or being withdrawn, aloof, cold, critical, judgmental or intolerant of self or others, having a fear of closeness, difficulty forming relationships, lack of empathy, and narcissism. Symptoms of heart chakra excess may be seen in smothering behavior, poor boundaries, codependency, and being overly self-sacrificing, demanding, insecure, and possessive.

Healing practices for the heart chakra include breathing exercises, working with the chest, shoulders and arms in expansion and contraction, opening up the space of the heart by rolling the shoulders back, examining assumptions and beliefs about relationships, and work around grief, forgiveness, emotional release, self-acceptance, and inner child healing.

Fifth Chakra

The *fifth* or *throat chakra* is the vibration and frequency of blue light, and controls and energizes the throat, the thyroid, and parathyroid glands. The developmental tasks of the fifth chakra are safe creative expression, balanced and assertive verbalization, the ability to speak one's truth appropriately, healthy communication skills, and symbolic thinking. This chakra expresses the basic rights to speak and be heard. Malfunctioning of this chakra may manifest physically in disorders of the throat, neck, ears and voice, tightness of the jaw, and toxicity to the body.

Traumas that adversely affect this chakra include being subjected to "lies, mixed messages, verbal abuse, constant yelling, [and] excessive criticism," being forced to keep secrets and threatened not to tell, and living with authoritarian, alcoholic or chemically dependent parents (Judith, 2004, p. 286). These types of abuses may cause deficiencies such as fear of speaking up or defending oneself, having a small or weak voice, lacking assertiveness, inability to communicate appropriately during conflict, difficulty expressing one's feelings, suffering from introversion and shyness, being tone deaf, and having poor rhythm. Symptoms of chakra excess are seen in an individual's unnecessary talking or talking as a defense or distraction, having a dominating voice, constantly interrupting, being inappropriately verbally aggressive toward others (particularly during conflict), being unable to listen, having poor auditory comprehension, and gossiping.

Healing practices that promote balance of the fifth chakra include exercises to loosen the neck and shoulders, singing, chanting, toning to release voice, journal writing, storytelling, acting or other creative expression, and psychotherapy with a focus on improvement of communication skills or inner child communication.

Sixth Chakra

The *forehead chakra* and the *ajna chakra*, located between the eyebrows, are treated separately in the energy system described by Sui (1990). The forehead chakra controls and energizes the pineal gland and the nervous system. Malfunctioning of this chakra may manifest as loss of memory, physical paralysis and epilepsy. The ajna chakra controls and energizes the pituitary gland and the endocrine system, which is involved in the regulation of the body's major organs. Malfunctioning of this chakra may manifest in diseases that relate to the endocrine glands and to the eyes.

Judith (2004) discusses the forehead and ajna chakra together as the *sixth* or *third eye chakra*, which is the vibration and frequency of purple or indigo light. The developmental tasks of the sixth chakra are the establishment of personal identity, the ability to recognize physical and symbolic patterns, and the development of intuitive knowing. This chakra expresses the basic right to see on all levels.

Conditions that adversely affect the functioning of the

sixth chakra are growing up in or living in a dangerous or frightening environment (e.g., war zone, trauma, violence), learning that what you see does not match what you are told, and the invalidation of your experience and of your intuitive knowing. These conditions may result in deficiencies such as poor memory, poor vision, insensitivity, difficulty perceiving a future or imagining alternatives, lack of imagination and visualization skills, difficulty remembering dreams, denial (refusal to see the truth of what's going on), and monopolarization (believing one true "right" way). These traumas may also cause chakra excesses including "hallucinations, delusions, obsessions, difficulty concentrating, [and] nightmares" (Judith, 2004, p. 339).

Healing practices that promote balancing of the sixth chakra include working to improve memory, connecting images with feeling, creating or studying visual art, art therapy, dream work, hypnosis, guided visualizations, and meditation.

Seventh Chakra

The *seventh* or *crown chakra* is the vibration and frequency of white or violet light, and is located at the top of the head. It controls and energizes the pineal gland, the brain, and the entire body. It is one of the major entry points of Ki energy into the body and H.E.F. Reiki treatment on the crown has the effect of connecting us to the Reiki source, divine consciousness itself, where we can receive spiritual guidance. According to Judith (2004), the developmental task of the seventh chakra is the assimilation of knowledge and the development of wisdom, open-mindedness, the ability to question, and capacity for thoughtful awareness. This chakra expresses the basic rights to know and learn. Physical problems of this chakra may manifest as migraines, brain tumors, amnesia, dementia, cognitive delusions or a coma.

According to Judith (2004), developmental traumas and abuses that adversely affect the balanced functioning of the seventh chakra include "withheld information, education that thwarts curiosity, forced religiosity, invalidation of one's beliefs," being denied the right to question or to think for oneself, being fed misinformation and lies, and spiritual abuse of any sort (p. 390). These abuses can result in deficiencies like "spiritual cynicism, learning difficulties, rigid belief systems, apathy, [and] excess in the lower chakras," which may be expressed through materialism, greed and domination of others (Judith, 2004, p. 391). Imbalances in the seventh chakra may also cause excesses like "over-intellectualization, spiritual addiction, mental confusion and dissociation from the body" (Judith, 2004, p. 391).

Healing practices that promote balancing of this chakra include unrestricted study and learning, spiritual discipline and balance, meditation practices to re-establish spiritual connection, and psychotherapy to help re-establish physical and mental-emotional connection and to modify dysfunctional and limiting thoughts and beliefs.

In summary, Ki energy animates and sustains life by flowing along energy pathways called meridians, through the major and minor chakras, and through the various levels of the H.E.F. Ki energy utilizes the chakras and energy channels to regulate mental and emotional functioning, to nourish the cells, tissues and organs of the body, and to support them in their functioning. When this flow is disrupted or diminished, the body-mind is adversely affected. Psychological conditions, physical illness and disease may result. Reiki treatments are helpful in eliminating energetic obstruction, in both deficient and excessive directions, and in reestablishing balanced flow and strength to the chakras and the levels of the H.E.F.

SYMPTOM FORMATION

The health of the physical body is directly related to the health of our cognitive, emotional, relational, and spiritual functioning. Stressful life events, physical, mental and emotional traumas, and repetitive negative environmental influences and conditioning all produce negative and self-defeating thoughts, beliefs, feelings, and behavior patterns. These negativities, conscious or not, remain as blocks or densities in the chakras and in the various levels of the H.E.F. If these elements are not cleared and released they will disrupt and block the flow of Ki. In turn, the disruption of Ki negatively affects the growth and development of healthy cells, tissue and body organs and interferes with the psychological functions that are regulated by the major chakras in the body. These negative elements and emotional holdings directly influence our psychological capacity to make meaning of ourselves, others and the world.

Sui (1990) states that negative elementals actually collect on the protective webs located at the base of major and minor chakras and affect the processing of incoming and outgoing Ki energy. He states that phobias are nothing more than traumatic fear energies or fearful thought energies that lodge in certain chakras. These fearful thoughts and feelings act as a "filter" through which we process new information. This "filter" maintains and sustains our negativity even in the face of positively changing circumstances. In other words, we create our own reality and project this onto the world and into the future, and thus perpetuate self-defeating thoughts, beliefs, feelings, and behavior patterns. The experiences of the past become our present and our future.

Four Major Points

It occurs to me that energy field theory suggests four major points regarding how symptoms function in the H.E.F. and how this influences our thinking about treatment.

Point 1

First, there is the idea that a field of energy permeates the body-mind, and that symptoms and conditions originate and are maintained in this field. Energy blocks and imbalances that underlie symptoms are most effectively treated by energy interventions that target this field. Reiki is one such energy that can do this. Reiki naturally seeks out the imbalance in a person on multiple levels and works to bring to the surface that which needs healing.

Because the different levels of the H.E.F. interpenetrate one another and reciprocally exchange information, body, mind, emotion and spirit affect one another and symptoms that originate on one level will eventually manifest on other levels as well. Problems are therefore multidimensional and may be found to have a mental part, an emotional part, a relational part, a physical part and a spiritual part. Valerie Hunt (1989), a scientist at UCLA who has been researching the H.E.F. for more than twenty-five years, found that imbalances between energy centers in a person's body and in the energy field correlated to certain kinds of disease. Thus, balancing and stabilizing the energy field and energy centers is a valuable part of treatment for any condition.

Clients often present with an awareness of one part but may not see others and may not see connections between them. If a client releases a blockage on one level but doesn't release related blockages on other levels, or doesn't change certain behavior patterns that are maintaining a blockage, then it is likely old problems will return or new problems could be created.

CASE EXAMPLES

I worked with a client who was very depressed but had little insight as to why. He was keenly aware of the emotional pain he experienced but unaware of the role his thinking was playing in it. I taught him how to watch his thoughts during Reiki treatments and he discovered patterns of self-defeating thinking that made him feel depressed. He also discovered the way these thoughts and feelings affected his body, and how he carried them in his posture. Further, he was able to see how all of this affected his relationships with others.

I was working with a man with irritable bowel syndrome (IBS) who came to me hoping that Reiki could relieve the physical pain and discomfort he had from the IBS. Reiki treatment didn't relieve his physical pain, but when other types of pain – mental, emotional and relational – surfaced, he became upset and didn't want to address these reactions. He stated that he only came to see me to work with his chronic physical pain.

I continued to see him for Reiki treatments, but because of his refusal to explore possible underlying reasons, his physical pain ultimately didn't change much and he stopped coming. He did not want to consider the idea that his physical pain could be connected to and related to his cognitive, emotional and relational functioning, and that healing was needed on more than one level.

Point 2

In traditional Western psychological perspectives, we are taught to identify who we are through the egoic mind, and that the mind is our essence. But from an energy perspective, we understand that subtle energy is our essence and that we are energy fields with physical, mental, emotional, relational and spiritual capacities. From this perspective we aren't the mind, we *have* a mind; we aren't the body, we *inhabit* a body; we aren't our emotions, we *have* emotions.

The practice of Reiki takes this energy perspective further by viewing our energetic essence as spiritually endowed consciousness itself. When we align ourselves with being consciousness, we can use the practice of mindfulness to observe our minds, our emotions and the functioning of our bodies.

One benefit of mindfulness is that it helps us to dis-identify with being the mind or even being our problems. Aligning with consciousness is being with our perceptions, without a "story." From an energy perspective, clients learn that they are not their problems and symptoms; they *have* problems and symptoms, and a story about them. By connecting to consciousness we connect to our in-born potential for transforming our symptoms and restoring balance.

Point 3

Because the H.E.F. is always in process and always in energetic relationship with others and the world, our psychological problems can be viewed as processes occurring in the present and not as static conditions located in the past, with which we are stuck. For example, from this perspective, a client is viewed as being in a process of depressing as opposed to being depressed. The idea that problems are processes makes them more amenable and accessible to strategies for change.

Point 4

Hunt's (1989) experiments also found that human energy fields are extremely responsive to intention. In her book *Infinite Mind*, Hunt (1989) discusses studies in which laying-on-of-hands healers greatly influenced the nature of the recipient's thoughts by what they themselves were thinking during a treatment. Based on her research, Hunt strongly suggests that hands-on healers communicate loving and healing intentions by way of their thoughts while treating others. Obviously, this principle applies to self-treatment as well. From the perspective of Psychotherapeutic Reiki, Hunt's (1989) research supports the idea that intentional energy interventions can be used to help clients alter the symptoms they carry.

In summary, problems and unresolved traumas, even from the distant past, are stored in the energy field and are expressing in the present. They are multi-dimensional, occurring across the various levels of the field, and can be seen as processes that are maintained by our relationships with others and the world. They are not static states. Furthermore, we can act upon the H.E.F. with our intention to release the effects of the past and bring about powerful and lasting change.

The above four points were instrumental in my conceptualization of the Four Therapeutic Tasks that are discussed in Chapter 3: Practicing Presence, Exploring the Body-Mind, Releasing and Clearing Energy Blocks, and Installing Corrective Experience:

- *Point 1* – Exploring the Body-Mind

- *Point 2* – Practicing Presence, Releasing and Clearing Energy Blocks

- *Point 3* – Practicing Presence, Releasing and Clearing Energy Blocks

- *Point 4* – Releasing and Clearing Energy Blocks, Installing Corrective Experience

In Chapters 3 through 8, issues and techniques are presented that incorporate these four points into practices for treating symptoms.

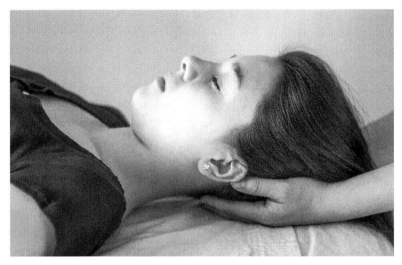

It is the therapist's responsibility to create and sustain a safe touch environment for herself and her clients.

Chapter 2

Issues with Touch in Psychotherapeutic Reiki

This chapter draws upon key points from *The Ethics of Touch* by Ben Benjamin and Cherie Sohnen-Moe (2003). Their book is an excellent resource for therapists using bodywork in their practices.

The primary method of transmitting Reiki is through the medium of touch and it is essential that the use of touch be made safe for both the client and the practitioner. Talking about the use of touch in psychotherapy evokes strong reactions from most therapists. In fact, even the subject of touch is taboo for many in today's culture.

There are several reasons that touch is such a provocative subject. First, our professional associations and organizations actively discourage the use of touch and warn us of sexual inappropriateness and misconduct. We practice in a professionally litigious culture and have developed a healthy fear of being sued or called before an Ethics Board. Second, we live in a low-touch culture that places little value on touch, and in fact, as we grow up we are indoctrinated with plenty of "hands-off" messages and messages that confuse the boundaries between sex, touch and intimacy.

Third, in Western healing professions there exists a body-mind split that suggests that the treatment of the body is in the province of medicine, physical therapy, massage therapy, etc., while psychotherapists treat the mind and psychological problems. Bodyworkers shouldn't counsel and psychotherapists shouldn't touch people. This split actively discourages therapists from being trained in the use of touch therapies, and from engaging in holistic forms of treatment.

Many therapists have come to believe that using touch in psychotherapy is unethical, but this is inaccurate. It is certainly unethical to be sexual in any way with clients, but the use of touch is not unethical in and of itself. However, using touch in your therapy practice does require special consideration of a number of important issues. At the most basic level it is the therapist's responsibility to create and maintain a safe treatment environment for himself and his clients. As Benjamin and Sohnen-Moe (2003) state, "The ethically safe touch experience does not just happen; it must be created, structured and sustained" (p. 134).

PREPARING AND PROTECTING YOURSELF

1.   Be trained in the highest level of Reiki training, the Master Level, before you offer Reiki in your therapeutic practice.

2.   Join a professional Reiki association and be versed

in their Codes of Ethics and Standards of Practice (see Appendix A).

> International Center for Reiki Training (ICRT)
> Telephone: (248) 948-8112
> Fax: (248) 948-9534
> Email: center@reiki.org
> Website: *www.reiki.org*

> International Association of Reiki Professionals (IARP)
> Telephone: (603) 881-8838
> Fax: (603) 882-9088
> Email: info@iarp.org
> Website: *www.iarp.org*

3. Obtain a malpractice insurance policy for the use of Reiki and touch. ICRT and IARP offer information about insurance policies on their websites, and Associated Bodywork and Massage Professionals offers a policy through its association.

> Associated Bodywork and Massage Professionals
> Telephone: (800) 458-2267
> Fax: (800) 667-8260
> Email: expectmore@abmp.com
> Website: *www.abmp.com*

4. Become affiliated with professional Reiki organizations. ICRT is William Rand's (1998) program in Southfield, MI, and they put out newsletters and news maga-

zines, sell supplies, and provide a membership listing for practitioners who are a part of ICRT. IARP also provides numerous resources for Reiki practitioners, including a magazine, job board, and educational and practice supplies.

5. Know your comfort level with touch and stay within your limits. If you decide to use hands-on Reiki, only work with those clients with whom you feel safe and only touch areas of the body you and your client are comfortable with (i.e., you can give a full Reiki treatment touching the head alone). If you want to use Reiki but not touch, you can send it to a client across the office, or you can attune clients or have them attuned by another Reiki professional so they can treat themselves.

6. From the onset of therapy, it is important to assess personality and risk factors. This hands-on approach is not appropriate for clients lacking sufficient ego strength, clients for whom touch is intrusive, constitutes boundary confusion or boundary violation, and clients prone to re-traumatization. Certain diagnostic categories (Post Traumatic Stress Disorder, personality disorders, major affective disorders, psychotic disorders) require more careful assessment to ensure that Reiki and touch are appropriate.

If the risks for transference, regression, triggering, acting out or eliciting sexual impulses are too great, do not make hands-on Reiki part of your treatment plan. You may decide that using Reiki would detract from or interfere with psychotherapy. Some clients need to keep psychotherapy and bodywork separate, for example to foster the building of better boundaries. It is important for the practitioner to think about when and why and how to introduce Reiki into the treatment process.

7. Create an environment of safety for your clients. Benjamin and Sohnen-Moe (2003) suggest the following parameters:

a. Maintain self-awareness regarding your thoughts, behaviors and interactions. Be clear about when you are inclined to flirt or place sexual energy on a situation, and be aware of how you engage your clients.

b. Be clear in your boundaries and intentions regarding relationships with your clients. Ethically, they should never be candidates for romantic interest, and it is important to respect those boundaries. Should romantic interest arise, it is important to seek out guidance from a mentor, supervisor or professional consultant.

c. Maintain a professional appearance and appropriate conduct during your sessions (i.e., don't wear revealing or provocative clothing, and monitor any potential mixed signals you might be sending).

d. Establish a professional treatment space with clear boundaries. Be aware that sight, sound, smell, touch, and imagination all have the potential to arouse. A professional atmosphere can help clarify boundaries and make your client feel safe.

e. Choose appropriate music and lighting, remembering that certain ambiances can be construed as seductive. In establishing a soothing atmosphere for a healing session, be aware of your choices and maintain professionalism.

f. Before working with a client, ask some standard questions of yourself. For example, ask yourself, "Is hands-on Reiki appropriate with this client? Am I the right person to do this? Do I need someone else present? What were my client's previous experiences with touch therapy like?"

g. Communicate in a professional manner using clinical terminology when necessary. Refrain from commenting on matters such as weight gain or loss and other appearance issues.

h. Be mindful of body contact during treatment, including how and where you touch, and whether you lean or brace yourself against the client without realizing it.

i. Treat all clients equally regardless of age, gender, or attractiveness.

j. Participate in on-going case consultation or supervision.

k. Keep thorough notes and document what occurs in each session.

Preparing and Protecting Your Client

If you and your client agree to make Reiki a part of your treatment plans, thoroughly orient your client to the use of Reiki and talk about what they can expect.

- Explain how Reiki works.

- Demonstrate the hand positions.

- Explain that clients stay fully dressed at all times and have the option of being covered by a blanket.

- Explain that there is no touch to sexual areas of the body.

- Instruct clients that they need to tell you if any touch becomes uncomfortable and that they have the right to discontinue any touch, at any time, on any part of the body.

- Go over the informed consent form and have the client sign. (See Appendix B.)

Reiki is often experienced as relaxing and pleasurable, but it can also elicit sexual arousal, physical discomfort, strong emotional reactions, and upsetting thoughts or memories, and you need to monitor and address these with your client. The practitioner needs to be attuned to the verbal and nonverbal communication a client gives and to monitor this throughout a treatment. For example, touch may cause a sexual response by triggering the parasympathetic nervous system that controls the sexual response, or the limbic system, causing an emotional response during or after a treatment.

A client may also interpret the meaning of the therapist's touch to be sexual depending on what parts of the body are touched, the duration and pressure of the touch, whether there was movement in the hands after contact was made, the gender of the practitioner and the client, how well the practitioner is known and trusted, and of course, the client's sexual history and experience. Regardless of the circumstances, if sexual arousal does occur on the part of either the practitioner or the client, it is always the practitioner's responsibility to address this and to establish and maintain appropriate boundaries.

The practitioner is responsible for responding nonsexually to the client and eliminating any misunderstanding on the client's part as to the intent of the treatment. If a misunderstanding or a boundary problem does arise, Benjamin and Sohnen-Moe (2003) recommend a procedure called the Intervention Model to help address this. Benjamin and Sohnen-Moe (2003) write:

> The Intervention Model is a communication model developed by Daphne Chellos, for practitioners to use when verbal or nonverbal communication from a client is unclear or when practitioners feel their boundaries are being violated. For instance, a situation in which a client expresses sexual interest requires a clear, unequivocal response that this is an inappropriate interest. This model also applies when a client is having an emotional reaction or release during a session, such as crying or expressing anger. (p. 125)

The following is a summary of the eight steps of the Intervention Model outlined by Benjamin and Sohnen-Moe (2003). You may need to go through all of them, or stop after one or two.

1. *Stop the treatment.* Using a firm demeanor, address the client with body language that is congruent with what you say, and make eye contact if possible.

2. *Describe the behavior.* State what you are observing (don't interpret): "I notice you look uncomfortable when I am near this area of the body."

3. *Clarify the client's experience.* Allow the client space to explain and wait for a clear answer rather than interpreting or jumping in.

4. *Educate the client if need be.* If a client has an unexpected physical response during a session, explain his experience so as to normalize it: "Sometimes clients feel aroused as a physiological response to touch, and this is a normal body response. But it is not my intent to cause sexual arousal."

5. *Re-state your intent.* Address and clarify the therapeutic contract so both you and the client feel safe: "My goal in this work is to…"

6. *Continue or discontinue session as appropriate.* Terminate the session if the client is acting inappropriately or sexually. If you are continuing the session, set conditions and clear parameters and have the client agree to them.

7. *Refer the client to other professionals as appropriate.* This is usually done after the session is over and you can have an open discussion and give your client the necessary referral information.

8. *Document the situation with a written record for*

your files. Discuss the situation with a supervisor if you have one, or obtain peer support.

Post Traumatic Stress Disorder

Reiki can be a very effective adjunct to psychotherapy for trauma survivors and clients suffering from PTSD:

1. It gives clients the experience of safe, non-sexual touch.

2. It helps clients reconnect to their bodies, increasing groundedness and relaxation in their bodies.

3. It helps reintegration of body memory by bringing out and releasing unprocessed body memory and feeling. Clients learn to experience and contain these memories and feelings safely. However, clients must be at a stage in their therapeutic process where they can safely handle touch and the feelings and body memories that touch may elicit.

According to Judith Herman (1992), there are three basic stages to the recovery process (as cited in Benjamin & Sohnen-Moe, 2003):

1. *Safety.* In this stage, the therapist helps the client establish physical and psychological safety. The client learns to ground into his body and establish control over it, and is able to meet basic physical needs (e.g., having a safe place to live, having safe people around him, eating well, sleeping well and exercising).

2. *Remembrance and mourning.* Once safety is established, the client can begin the process of remember-

ing and integrating unconscious, fragmented and buried memories. This usually sinks the client into intense grief and mourning. It is important to remember that it is in the recollection, sharing and mourning of his story that the client can move toward assimilation and healing.

3. *Reconnection.* In the third stage of recovery, the client begins to experience an integrated, intact self. He remembers and recognizes his trauma, but is not controlled by it, and is able to more healthily connect to others and the world.

According to Benjamin and Sohnen-Moe (2003), it is generally safe to start touch therapy and bodywork when the client is in Stage 3, although it may also be helpful with Stage 2 issues if the client's symptoms are manageable.

Boundaries

Practitioners need to be very sensitive to the boundaries of touch before, during, and after treatment with survivors. For example, when greeting or saying goodbye, do you shake hands? Do you put your hand on the client's shoulder or back? Do you hug the client? These are all things to think about and talk about with your client.

The boundaries of survivors have been so abused that they may be unaware of being violated, or are unable to protect themselves by saying no to unwanted touch if they are aware. With survivors, the range of physical contact on and off the table must be handled extremely carefully. I once worked with a client who enjoyed hands-on Reiki treatments but did not like goodbye hugs; to her this was too intimate and triggering. For some clients, the context of touch in a hug is very different than the context of touch in a standard Reiki treatment.

Body Memories

Memories appear along a continuum of consciousness ranging from an integrated memory to a brief, faint recollection that is gone in an instant (un-integrated memory) to a flashback, which is out of the person's control.

Touch and Reiki treatment on any part of the body may trigger memory, as the body stores memory in the cells of the tissue. The most sensitive parts of the body for trauma survivors are of course the genitals, breasts and buttocks, but also the mouth, throat, neck, chest, abdomen, and front, back and inner thighs. The type of memory triggered may be one that is already understood and accepted (pleasant or painful), or it could be a painful memory that causes an upsurge of emotion, but emotion that is safe for the client to feel and express. In the case of this type of emotional release, although the emotion may be strong and the release dramatic, the client is able to stay present and contain her experience.

Case Example

I had a client who experienced a powerful body memory and emotional release while I was giving Reiki to the base of her throat. She suddenly remembered almost drowning as a young child when she fell into a swimming pool. Over the course of several sessions she was able to work through this traumatic memory and release its effects.

Flashbacks

A flashback is the experience of reliving or re-experiencing a traumatic event as if it were occurring in the present. Benjamin and Sohnen-Moe (2003) write, "When a flashback is triggered, concrete and distinct memories suddenly surface and intrude on the present" (p. 231). The client is awake but out of the need for psychological protection, becomes dissociated, exhibiting intense emotional reactions such as fear, trembling, shaking and dilated pupils. Her eyes are unfocused and she may cry, curl up in a ball on the table, or refuse to respond when asked a question.

Generally, as a self-protective measure, the client has left her body and is out of touch with the present and present-day feelings, thoughts and sensations. She may experience numbness or talk incoherently (e.g., saying things like, "Who are you? What are you doing? Get away from me.").

Benjamin and Sohnen-Moe (2003) instruct that when a flashback occurs, the task of the therapist is to bring the client back to the present as safely and quickly as possible. The following is a summary of their steps for retrieving a client from a flashback:

1. Immediately break contact with your hands and

call the client's name: "Sandra, can you hear me?" Note that this situation is different than an emotional release, where you would not break contact but would continue to be with the client during the release. If it is a flashback, the client might not reply or would respond in a way that is unusual for her.

2.   Continue to make voice contact in an effort to orient the client to the present: "Sandra, this is Richard and you are here in my office."

3.   Ask questions to help ground the client: "Do you know where you are? Are you here with me?"

4.   Make eye contact if possible. Encourage the client to open her eyes and focus either on you or on an object in the room to help bring her back to the present.

5.   Cover the client with a blanket to create a safe physical boundary. Stand to the side of the table to give the client space.

6.   Encourage the client to sit up. If you have the impulse to help, ask the client if it's all right to touch her. Do not touch the client without permission.

7.   Pull up a chair, but don't sit too close, and don't sit higher than the client. Ensure that you are in a position relative to the client that feels safe to her.

8.   If you discussed the possibility of a flashback ahead of time, follow the client's instructions on what else would be helpful at this time.

9.   Ask the client if she is feeling numbness in any part

of the body, especially her legs. Numbing indicates that the effects of the flashback were particularly strong and are still occurring. This is important information for you to have as you both move forward in the session.

10. Once the client has sufficiently recovered and is stable, take time to talk about what happened in the session. Don't probe for details of the flashback; rather, allow the client space to share what she is ready to share.

11. When she is ready, process why the flashback occurred. Was she triggered by something you said, a touch on a specific part of the body, the background music, or something else? Gather as much information as you can in a non-invasive way.

12. If you both elect to continue the session, check in with the client frequently to ensure that she is fully present. Be aware of the client becoming spacey or beginning to feel numb anywhere, particularly in the legs.

13. After the session, sit and talk with the client to help her gain closure on the experience. Ask her what was and was not helpful in assisting her back to the present, and if appropriate, establish a plan of action should this occur again during a future session.

14. Ask about the client's plans after leaving your office. She should be with a person with whom she feels safe. If the client is too disoriented to travel, help her get a taxi or call someone to pick her up. Most people recover from a flashback within one half hour of coming back to the

present, but some take longer. Establish a plan to follow should another flashback occur once she leaves your office (whom she should call, etc.).

In summary, it is the therapist's responsibility to create and sustain the safe touch experience for himself and his client. This requires careful assessment, planning and the co-participation of the client. In the event that touch becomes invasive or triggering, the therapist needs to stop the treatment, address the problem, and determine the appropriate next course of action.

Just as water in the physical world flows when unimpeded and is "blocked" or "stuck" when obstructed, so too can Ki become blocked in the body and H.E.F., which can generate symptoms.

CHAPTER 3

Treatment Concepts and Therapeutic Tasks

Psychotherapeutic Reiki understands psychological health as the unimpeded flow of energy in the H.E.F. Humans cultivate and maintain psychological health by being able to release and clear the negative effects of any traumatic experience or set of conditions that occur in their lives as development unfolds. However, just as water in the physical world flows when unimpeded and is "blocked" or "stuck" when obstructed, so too can energy become blocked in the body and in the H.E.F. When an individual is unable to release the effects of negative conditioning or traumatic experience, the flow of Ki energy in the body and the field becomes depleted, congested, blocked, disrupted or disturbed in ways that produce energetic imbalance. This imbalance can eventually affect the nature and quality of our thoughts, beliefs, feelings, moods, behavior and physical health.

When I initially meet with a client, I spend several sessions gathering data for a standard evaluation. I take a history of the presenting problem and of the person's background. I look for any unusual experiences, traumas or losses and the core beliefs that these experiences have created. I note predominant moods and difficult emotional states, recurrent relationship problems, medical problems, chronic pain issues, addictions and behavioral problems.

The client and I discuss the presenting problem as an energetic event occurring on and across all levels of the H.E.F. – physical, emotional, mental, interpersonal and spiritual – and based on this information, we develop a treatment plan and goals and discuss particular issues to target with the use of Reiki. A target is a specific symptom or symptom cluster related to the presenting problem, such as a negative and self-limiting belief like "I'm such a loser," an unresolved traumatic memory, a recurring or troubling emotional state (such as anxiety, anger or sadness), chronic pain, a negative behavior pattern, an addiction, or energy blocks and energetic imbalance.

The decision to use Reiki in the treatment process depends on several factors:

1. The client's desire and willingness;

2. Safety and appropriateness of the use of touch; and

3. Reiki's usefulness with the presenting problem AND with treatment goals.

If a client and I decide to use Reiki as a part of the treatment process, the first thing I do is explain how Reiki works and what she can expect from a treatment. I demonstrate the hand positions, discuss any sensitivity around touch, and review and have the client sign the informed consent form. I answer any questions the client may have about Reiki to the best of my ability.

The decision to use Reiki in any given session is determined session by session and case by case. There are times when the client and I spend the entire session talking and working in traditional ways. At other times, we use Reiki for part or all of the session, for any of the following reasons.

• If a talk session is particularly stressful or brings out a strong emotional reaction, it is often helpful to give the client Reiki for the last ten to fifteen minutes to help him de-stress, feel grounded or integrate any new awareness.

• If a primary goal is stress reduction or relaxation training, we will use Reiki in conjunction with other techniques on a regular basis for most of the session. At the end of each session we briefly process the experience and what can be learned from it.

• If we want to work on a particular target that was defined at intake or that comes up in a particular session, we will utilize Reiki.

• If we want the Reiki to work on the issue being discussed, I give Reiki while the client and I talk, and again briefly process the experience at the end of the session.

• If I find that the Reiki treatments are helping, I will often attune the client to Reiki so that he can use Reiki on himself between sessions. This not only facilitates the healing process but also gets the client more involved in the treatment, and it empowers him by giving him a resource for self-care.

Reiki and Spiritual Guidance in the Treatment Process

Reiki is defined as spiritually guided life force energy. It is the God consciousness, Rei, which guides the life force energy, Ki, in the practice of Reiki. Reiki has a divine intelligence that can reveal, illuminate and treat the underlying causes of a problem on any level of the H.E.F. Reiki connects us to our vital energy and spirit, and can increase our awareness and insight.

Reiki is a method that emerged from Buddhist spirituality and practice, and like Buddhist spiritual practices it focuses on being and being present, on connecting with our Buddha nature, divine consciousness itself, and on opening our awareness to our moment-to-moment experience just as it is. Clients who meditate frequently tell me that the experience of Reiki is similar to sitting in mindfulness meditation. In fact, it is interesting to note that in his Reiki classes, Dr. Mikao Usui, the founder of Reiki practices, taught a method of mindfulness meditation called Gassho Meditation and encouraged his students to practice meditation in the morning and in the evening (Usui & Petter, 1999).

Reiki quiets the mind, calms the body and opens the heart as it brings our awareness into the present. It promotes acceptance, insight, balance, relief, and release. As Reiki awakens our capacity to observe the body-mind, it allows our attention to be more easily focused. Reiki creates an environment in which the body-mind comes into a state of refined subtle energy and awareness, and it is in this heightened state of awareness that the body-mind accesses its healing potential, releases energetic obstructions, and vitalizes the body.

When Usui developed his Reiki system and began teaching students in Japan in the 1920s, he taught the use of specific hand positions for treating specific disorders and a method for using one's intuition to guide the treatment process. In this intuitive method, the practitioner aligned himself with the spiritual Reiki source at the start of the treatment and asked for guidance to provide the most effective healing for the client. The practitioner then followed the intuitive guidance he received to decide what hand positions to use in treating the client (Usui & Petter, 1999).

Usui also taught that once a practitioner was attuned to Reiki, Reiki not only flowed through her hands but also through her breath, her eyes, and her intention. Any or all of these ways of transmitting Reiki could be used in the treatment process. In the course of a treatment the practitioner might be intuitively led to lay hands on, tap, stroke, blow on, and use her vision to treat the client's body as she felt directed to do so. In the intuitive method of Usui, practitioners learned to attune to the Reiki source and to trust the spiritual guidance and intuition they received about where and how to treat the client (Usui & Petter, 1999).

This intuitive way of working was lost when Hawayo Takata brought Reiki to the Western world in 1938. Although she taught her students to begin treatment with an opening prayer and connection to the Reiki source, she prescribed a series of standardized hand positions to be used by practitioners during a Reiki treatment, regardless of the disorder being treated. It is not clear why she departed from Usui's method, but for whatever reason, Takata's approach has become the predominant way that Reiki is used and taught in the West today (Usui & Petter, 1999). In my experience, both approaches are effective and both recognize that Reiki spiritual guidance is working through the practitioner in the practice of Reiki. In my Reiki classes, I teach students both the Takata and the intuitive methods so that students can experience each style.

By opening our awareness and attention to the flow of Reiki, we connect with the Reiki source, divine consciousness and our shared Buddha nature, and to the healing this can bring. We allow ourselves to be guided to the issues and to the places that most need healing in the client. We may intuitively "see" with our inner vision, feel the presence of a saint, spirit guide or other being giving their blessings or direction, receive a message in thought form, be directed by the sensations flowing through our hands or just know through our intuition where healing is needed.

Many psychotherapists are trained to assess, diagnose and direct the treatment process. They are trained to be in charge. Consequently, it can be unfamiliar and a challenge to allow the Reiki to guide them in the treatment process. What is required is a balancing act between using our ideas and using our intuition. In the practice of Psychotherapeutic Reiki, practitioners alternate between directing and receiving intuitive direction. We develop a target to work on, apply Reiki and use what the Reiki brings up to guide the next step in the therapy. We use both traditional talk therapy strategies and Reiki in order to treat the client's symptoms and restore balance and harmony.

This process expresses an ongoing dialectical relationship between talk therapy and Reiki. One informs the other and suggests which direction to go toward resolving the client's symptoms and condition, whether it is treating depression, modifying cognition, practicing a new behavior or using Reiki techniques to release the effects of unresolved trauma.

I use Reiki by itself and in conjunction with certain therapeutic techniques to target and treat particular problems, issues and areas of blockage in the H.E.F. Reiki energy empowers these techniques. It guides, reveals, clarifies, and intensifies their effects. Reiki is very responsive to the intention set by the practitioner and the client and can be directed toward a particular problem. I have discovered that Reiki is particularly helpful in treating symptoms that develop as a result of body-mind disconnection, held trauma energy, stress, and chronic pain.

Four Therapeutic Tasks

As I began using Reiki in my psychotherapy practice, I thought of it as a stress reduction exercise that could help clients focus their attention on their symptoms and learn to relax around them. Over the course of time and as I experimented with the use of Reiki, I found that there were four particular ways that Reiki was helpful in the treatment of psychological problems and conditions. Reiki helped people to relax around their symptoms in the present; it promoted insight; it assisted in letting go of unwanted symptoms; and it helped in the creation of new healing perspectives.

I realized that the Reiki techniques I was developing and practicing easily fell into one of these four self-selected categories. I began to think of these categories as therapeutic tasks and noticed that they usually followed one another sequentially, although there are particular symptoms that require more time and focus on one task over others. Ultimately, I came to identify these Four Therapeutic Tasks as Practicing Presence, Exploring the Body-Mind, Releasing and Clearing Energy Blocks, and Installing Corrective Experience.

Practicing Presence

The first task, *Practicing Presence*, is about the relationship clients have with their symptoms. Although it is understandable to want to minimize, deny or distance ourselves from our symptoms out of judgment, fear or pain, in many cases this only serves to intensify them and obscure their meaning. Practicing Presence is the experience of allowing our symptoms to be as they are. It involves the use of techniques for helping clients stay present with their symptoms in a non-judgmental and self-accepting manner while receiving Reiki. Practicing Presence with Reiki works to reduce a client's symptom by reducing his resistance to the symptom.

Practicing Presence helps the client to develop a level of skill at staying present with the moment-to-moment experience of her symptoms. To do this requires a transition from our normal "thinking or doing" mode to one of observing. As Jon Kabat-Zinn (1994) writes in *Wherever You Go, There You Are*, being present means shifting into the "being" mode: "Think of yourself as an eternal witness, as timeless. Just watch this moment, without trying to change it at all. What is happening? What do you feel? What do you see? What do you hear?" (p. 11).

This therapeutic task is helpful in treating symptoms of body-mind disconnection, anxiety and cognitive distortions because it helps to anchor awareness in the body instead of the mind. When working with this first task, it is helpful to instruct clients to hold an attitude of mindfulness while receiving Reiki. I ask them to be aware of their present experience with an attitude of acceptance toward whatever sensations, thoughts or feelings arise (Kabat-Zinn, 1994).

When you are using Practicing Presence to look more deeply into a symptom, a sample instruction to give is: "Quiet your mind, open your heart and connect to the inner energy of the body. Know that your body holds wisdom about the nature of your symptoms and can give you the awareness and insight you need."

When we are present with ourselves and our experience without trying to deny, resist or dissociate, we create more space and acceptance around our symptoms and we open to the potential for transforming them. Diane Shainberg (2000) writes in *Chasing Elephants*, "In Buddhist teachings on wisdom, leaving things as they are brings forth our radiant, open presence. And when we are in touch with this presence, we act with wisdom and trust that things in our life will transform in a most intelligent way" (p. xv).

I have found it helpful to introduce the body scan (Kabat-Zinn, 1990) described in Chapter 4 and breath work as techniques for increasing the client's ability to be present. The combination of Reiki, mindfulness, body scanning and abdominal breathing can greatly reduce stress and facilitate healing. These techniques can alter a person's experience of herself and her relationship to her symptoms. They can increase a person's ability to tolerate discomfort, develop greater self-control, and develop a non-reactive acceptance of her experience with the body-mind.

Benefits of Practicing Presence with Reiki:

•   Practicing Presence brings us into conscious and sensory contact with the H.E.F.

•   Clients can connect to the aliveness of the inner energy field of the body and feel the way this energy animates the physical body.

- Clients learn to be present with their symptoms in a calm, non-judgmental and abiding manner.

- Clients who frequently dissociate from their body can learn to connect in a safe, non-threatening way through the peaceful energy of Reiki.

- Reiki elicits the body's natural relaxation response, which effectively combats stress reactions.

- Reiki increases body awareness and body-mind connection.

- Reiki also brings awareness to clients' symptoms and to the mind's reactions to those symptoms.

- Clients learn to access the body-mind's innate capacity to heal itself.

EXPLORING THE BODY-MIND

The second task, *Exploring the Body-Mind*, takes being present a step further by investigating the client's symptoms more fully. While the client's symptoms or condition are present, we explore the nature and quality of his thinking, the emotions he is having in relationship to his symptoms, and the sensations he is feeling in the body and where they are located. Exploratory techniques examine the origin and meaning of the symptoms he is carrying.

When Reiki is directed into the body-mind, into the H.E.F., it encounters not only our symptoms but also the unresolved, unaccepted, un-integrated issues of our lives. As this happens, Reiki brings these symptoms and issues up and into clearer focus in order to move toward releasing them. Reiki may calm and soothe the client's symptoms or intensify their effects, depending on what's needed to treat the symptoms. For one client the Reiki immediately brings out tension, for another an emotional reaction, while still others may feel relaxed and de-stressed.

One way of using exploratory techniques is for the practitioner to give Reiki to the client while the client brings a problem to mind. For example, an unresolved trauma memory, a problematic thought or belief, or a negative feeling state that troubles her can all be explored with this technique. The practitioner has the client notice, explore and describe the effects in her body-mind. This helps the client develop a fuller picture of the problem and facilitates understanding and insight. It teaches the client to attend to and stay with her experience of what's occurring in the body-mind rather than turning away from it.

At other times these techniques are an investigation into the relationship between the present moment and the past. When we open our awareness to the symptoms we hold, we are encountering the effects of the past that persist in the present. These techniques help us discover the origin of the problem, separate the past from the present, and make problems more workable.

Benefits of Exploring the Body-Mind with Reiki:

• Exploring the Body-Mind takes Practicing Presence a step further by actively investigating clients' symptoms.

- Exploratory techniques can increase clients' symptom tolerance.

- Reiki promotes clients' body-mind healing by increasing awareness of the physical, emotional, mental, relational, and spiritual aspects of a symptom.

- Reiki can bring understanding and insight into the origin and meaning of symptoms.

RELEASING AND CLEARING ENERGY BLOCKS

The third task, *Releasing and Clearing Energy Blocks*, involves the use of techniques for letting go of held trauma energy and painful memories, thoughts and emotions, and for releasing the energetic charge underlying them. On a psychological level, we release the power of an erroneous belief by seeing through it, and we release the power of toxic emotion by connecting it with its original source. On an energetic level, Reiki counters the power of a mental or emotional symptom by releasing the underlying energetic charge. This level of intervention targets the etheric body, which stores and carries symptoms. Clearing and release techniques work on the principle that while Ki vitalizes symptoms, Reiki can de-vitalize them, especially with attention and intention.

Before painful memories, thoughts and emotions can be released they need to be experienced, recognized and accepted. They need to be brought out into the open and this can initially intensify their effects. Therefore, release work requires that the client feels safe enough in his body to tolerate the experience of strong emotional reactions and troubling thoughts, images and memories, and the therapist needs to assess the client's ability to do this. Practicing Presence and Exploring the Body-Mind are very helpful in preparing the client for release work.

There are several techniques used for releasing underlying energy charges when the client is ready, such as directed attention and balancing and vitalizing chakras (Chapter 4), the Mental-Emotional Release Technique (Chapter 6), and aura clearing and sweeping (Chapter 8). For a complete list, please refer to the Index of Techniques at the back of this book.

Benefits of Releasing and Clearing with Reiki:

• Reiki brings up symptoms in order to help release them.

• Reiki helps to release the energy charge underlying stress reactions, negative emotional states, held trauma energy, and intrusive thoughts and memories.

• Reiki clears energy blocks and restores the free and healthy flow of Ki in the energy field.

• Reiki is an effective approach for pain management, as it can ease acute and chronic pain. It is being used as an effective complement to pain medication and other therapies in hospitals around the country, particularly in oncology centers.

Installing Corrective Experience

The fourth task, *Installing Corrective Experience*, is predicated on the understanding that our thoughts ultimately create our reality, and that once aware of this, we can work to change our experiences in this world. This is discussed in more detail in Chapter 5. This task involves the use of techniques for starting to think, feel and act differently and with positive intention. Reiki not only helps to release the energetic charge underlying unresolved trauma and negative conditioning, it also supplies a positive energetic charge to corrective experiences. When the practitioner holds a healing intention in concert with the client, their energetic fields merge. In this way, the practitioner is assisting the client in letting go of the symptom and establishing a corrective experience.

Techniques in this category seek to input new information into the client's body-mind and energy field. After clients have released blockages, this new information is installed in the form of affirmations, positive images, successful outcomes, corrective thoughts and beliefs, and positive feelings that promote states of healing, happiness, contentment, and well-being. These can be conceptualized as transformational intentions or healing prescriptions. We replace painful thoughts, judgments and beliefs with positive, loving and compassionate messages. As Jack Kornfield (2008) writes in *The Wise Heart*, we "create a true antidote, a phrase or two or three, that completely transforms the falsehood of these unhealthy thoughts" (p. 306).

Benefits of Installing Corrective Experience with Reiki:

• Reiki energetically supports the replacement of negative conditioning with positive, self-selected and self-directed ideals.

• Reiki supports the installation of corrective affirmations, emotions, imaginings, and intentions.

• Reiki promotes rebalancing of the energy field by inputting new information to improve mental, emotional and physical well-being.

A Four-Step Protocol

One treatment approach is to use the four tasks in sequence while working with a client on a particular symptom or symptom cluster. This may be done in one session or over the course of many sessions, depending upon the nature of the problem and how pervasive it is. For example, in working with states of anxiety or panic, the first task would be to give the client Reiki while having him practice being present with the anxiety and other related symptoms (e.g., shallow breathing, muscular tension, fearful thoughts, nausea, etc.). The therapist encourages the client to hold an attitude of acceptance around these distressing symptoms while allowing himself to fully feel them, understanding that he is safe at all times.

Once the client is able to achieve a higher degree of presence and tolerance for the anxiety symptoms, the client and therapist begin the task of exploring the anxiety more fully. One method of exploring is to ask descriptive questions such as:

- *Where is this feeling of anxiety located in your body?*

- *If it had a shape, what shape would it be?*

- *What color, size, texture, weight is it?*

- *If the anxiety had a voice, what would it say? Does it have anything to say to you?*

- *What does it need from you right now?*

- *Do you have anything you want to say to it?*

- *Are there other emotions associated with it?*

- *Are there any memories or images connected with it?*

The purpose of this exploration is to increase the client's awareness and connection to his anxiety and to discover more fully the meaning that it holds.

The third task is to work on releasing the anxiety and the energetic charge underlying any specific memory or thought pattern that the exploration brought up. After releasing as much of the anxiety as possible, the final step is to install corrective thoughts, feelings or images that work to counter the source of the client's anxiety.

Certain problems and symptoms will require the focus of one of the four tasks more than the others. It isn't always necessary or appropriate to use them all, or to use them in order. For example, I have had clients who need to practice being present for many months and others who are immediately ready for release work.

CASE EXAMPLE

Melissa was seeking Psychotherapeutic Reiki for help with symptoms of anxiety, panic, feelings of inadequacy and intimidation in social situations. She attributed these symptoms to growing up in an alcoholic home where there was a lot of anger and angry outbursts, alternating with emotional distance and neglect of her needs. She had been in psychotherapy for a lot of her adult life and had made progress, but still struggled with troubling symptoms. She had heard of Reiki and hoped that this energy work could help further her healing.

Melissa spent several sessions working with the first or basic task of Practicing Presence. She had tried meditation in the past but found that she was too restless to stay with it for very long. She found the experience of Reiki to be soothing, quieting and relaxing. She started learning to identify and track bodily sensations, images, thoughts, and feelings that came and went during the Reiki treatments. She became more comfortable in and connected to her body.

Melissa had more difficulty when we began working on the second task, exploring her symptoms. For example, while I gave her Reiki, I asked her to focus on her childhood and to describe what it had been like growing up in her family. Remembering her past brought up strong emotion, unhappy memories, critical beliefs about herself and her parents, and feelings of shame about herself. She had come to blame herself for things she had had no control over. The Reiki helped to pair relaxation with the emotion she felt as she talked about the past. As she did this her anxiety lessened.

As we explored her narrative, we chose several issues to target for release work: releasing feelings of self-blame, shame and inadequacy, releasing the charge underlying several particularly intrusive memories, and releasing her fear of re-traumatization by present relationships. Over the course of several months, I used the Mental-Emotional Release Technique to help Melissa discharge emotion and decrease the intensity of those feelings and memories.

We then began to work on the fourth task, installing corrective beliefs about herself and about her capabilities. In this phase, the client and therapist develop affirmations and healing scenes to install in the client's chakras and energy field. In Melissa's case, we installed healthy replacements for dysfunctional scenes, along with healing affirmations such as, "I am safe and secure in the present," "I am lovable as I am," and "I am free of the traumatic effects of my past." The energy work we did took place over the course of several years and was interspersed with traditional talk therapy sessions.

Symptoms as Process and Function

Melissa's symptoms have several causes: they are learned and habitual patterns of response to psychological injury, they are expressions of unreleased mental and emotional pain, and they are efforts to avoid re-traumatization. These symptoms express Melissa's attempt to adapt to unresolved trauma and to the unfinished business of her childhood pain. They are the body-mind's effort to find some degree of stability in the face of destabilizing conditions.

From a systems perspective, the H.E.F. can be conceptualized as a system of interactive parts (physical, emotional, mental, relational, spiritual) that are constantly seeking to maintain physical and psychological homeostasis in response to ever-changing conditions. Symptoms express through these parts and through their interconnections and interactions, and are vitalized by the flow of Ki on the energy level of the H.E.F.

Symptoms limit the system's ability to function optimally and when they persist, the system is forced to adapt to this state of imbalance. Our symptoms actually keep us in a state of disequilibrium that, unless corrected, becomes habitual. Over time, this state becomes our new "normal," a chronic state of imbalance. This adaptation is particularly true when symptoms develop in childhood and persist into adult life.

Our symptoms become a part of our everyday experience; they are a part of how we live our lives. They become an aspect of our self-definition and our identity, and they are reflected in the way we treat ourselves and others (e.g., "I'm just an anxious person," "I just don't trust people," "I'm not as emotionally strong or capable as others," or "I'm not that smart"). Without the self-acceptance of these perceived limitations and the protection they afford, we actually believe we could be worse off, that we might not be able to function. As a former professor of mine, Dr. Leon Brenner, used to say, "It's better to have a crutch and hop than to be unable to walk."

Although the mind tends to solidify symptoms and make them into "things," symptoms are not static conditions; they are energy flow and process. They are actions, energy movements of thought, movements of emotion expressing in the present. Instead of stating, "I am depressed," it is more accurate to say, "I am depressing," and it is more helpful to ask, "How am I depressing at this moment? How am I managing to perpetuate my symptoms, to keep them active?" This approach is more descriptive and less analytical. It is directed at the way a symptom is constructed, examining the how, what and where of a symptom, the function the symptom serves and how it is disrupting energy flow.

Symptoms can serve several different functions:

• Symptoms are the expression of *blocked*, *excessive* or *deficient* Ki in the chakras and energy levels of the H.E.F. A client struggling with chronic anxiety is likely experiencing an energetic deficiency in feeling emotionally safe and secure and an excess of Ki in being fearful and worried.

These imbalances are stored in the body and H.E.F. and can be detected and balanced with Reiki treatments. For example, Reiki can be used to strengthen certain thought patterns and lessen others. It can add a positive charge to healing affirmations, and can release the negative charge underlying strong emotion.

• Symptoms can represent an *overcorrection* by the system to restore equilibrium and balance to a state that pre-existed an energetic disturbance. For example, following a traumatic event, the symptoms of anxiety and hypervigilance serve the goal of avoiding re-traumatization. After a loss, depressive symptoms may keep a person from developing hope and thus protect him from the potential of a future loss. The problem is that these efforts either intensify the existing symptom or create new ones. To restore balance means to see this adaptive effort clearly and to be able to see through it. It means recognizing the tendencies of the mind and working to transform them.

• Symptoms can be the expression of *outdated, habitual response patterns* that are persisting in the present. No matter how uncomfortable the symptoms are, they are familiar so we habituate to them. To restore balance means to release the effects of the past and release outdated patterns.

• Symptoms can be a response to mental, emotional or physical pain made worse by *resistance* to this pain. Resistance to pain is often the system's attempt to get rid of it by denying, suppressing or overcoming it. To restore balance means to meet our resistance with understanding, increased compassion and acceptance.

•   Symptoms can be created by *imbalances* that exist between the heart, mind, emotion, and body. For example, when the egoic mind is upset by the body's experience of emotional or physical pain, it reacts to this pain with fear-producing thoughts and judgments, which can actually intensify the pain. To restore equilibrium means to rebalance the relationships between the heart, mind, emotion, and body. In this case, it is important to hold the mind in compassion and loving kindness in order to ease its suffering. We do this by sending heart energy into the mind while giving Reiki.

While our symptoms can be understood as the system's effort to balance, protect and adapt, they do so at a price. They generally narrow our range of functioning and disrupt the flow of Ki, which among other things negatively affects the health of the physical body. When we understand our symptoms to be the body-mind's effort to adapt and establish stability, then it becomes important to investigate how it is doing this.

As we investigate the meaning and function of a symptom, we can ask questions such as the following:

•   *How is this symptom adaptive?*

•   *How is the symptom trying to restore balance?*

•   *What is its function?*

- *What messages is it carrying from the past?*

- *What beliefs does this symptom hold?*

- *What emotions, memories or images does this symptom express?*

- *Where is the symptom being carried in the body?*

- *How is the symptom resisting the present?*

- *What would happen if this symptom did not exist?*

Ultimately, restoring balance means being free of our conditioning, finishing unfinished business so we can meet each moment as the new moment it is. Restoring balance means to live in the present, to open to life on life's terms with self-compassion, acceptance and non-resistance. When we are able to open to how things actually are, our symptoms often begin to transform.

BALANCING AND HEALING

The Four Therapeutic Tasks are ways of bringing balance and healing to the body, to the mind, to the heart, to emotional pain and to relationship issues. Healing is not necessarily curing, and trying to cure a symptom and trying to heal a symptom are very different approaches to treatment.

From the perspective of curing, the symptom is viewed as the problem and the goal of treatment is to remove it and return the client to a pre-symptom state. Healing, on the other hand, is focused on bringing the client into a greater state of wholeness, whether the symptom is cured or not. For some clients, this means trying to live with certain intractable symptoms with greater ease and acceptance (e.g., symptoms due to chronic pain, complex PTSD, biochemically-based psychological disorders).

Healing is coming into an accepting presence with our symptoms and meeting them with positive thoughts, soothing emotions, and open-hearted compassion. Thus, a primary goal of healing is to rebalance the relationship the client has toward his symptoms. Rebalancing begins by having the client enter into the symptom as it is and investigate its nature and meaning. As Levine (1987) writes, "By softly exploring and letting go of the resistance which tightly encompasses discomforts in the mind/body, the next level is uncovered and our pain becomes yet more accessible to healing" (p. 65). Often, it is from this exploration that treatment options emerge: attending, allowing, accepting, modifying, releasing, intentioning, replacing.

Healing is a process of being with a symptom and gently moving it in the direction of a more balanced state, even when that state isn't the complete cessation of that symptom. When a client's symptoms are the result of his conditioning, it is unlikely that the treatment process will fully eradicate the symptom. You cannot simply eliminate the conditioning that your life situation and circumstances have produced. You can however, bring a more accepting and soothing presence to these effects. A client may never be free of anxiety caused by childhood trauma, but his relationship to it can be modified in such a way as to lessen the intensity and duration of it and make it more manageable to live with. The lessening of anxiety creates a restoration of balance in his life, one in which anxiety plays a less debilitating role.

Reiki, mindfulness, heartfulness, and self-compassion practices ease our symptoms and move them in more healing directions. Their action is not to oppose a symptom, but to accept and work with it. Resisting a psychological or emotional problem only succeeds in suppressing it. This suppression is fatiguing and often the problem will re-emerge over time, sometimes with more intensity or severity.

Resisting a symptom is analogous to fighting a white water current that is pulling you down a rushing river: the more you fight against a current the more fatigued you become, but if you don't resist the flow of water and instead allow yourself to ride along with it, you can begin to edge yourself towards the safety of the shore. Healing is like this. Healing is a process of being with our symptoms and not fighting against them. As we bring presence to our symptoms and work with them, we can gently move towards their transformation.

Healing Perspectives that Help to Restore Balance

• Coming into presence with how things are, seeing clearly and looking more deeply into the nature and function of our symptoms.

• Supporting a symptom's transformation through the use of positive attention and intention.

• Balancing the energies of the mind and body with

the energy of the heart. Approaching our symptoms with the resources that the heart can offer (see Chapter 7).

• Relating *to* our symptoms rather than reacting *from* them. When we react from our symptoms, we close down. When we relate to them, we open up.

• Bringing a spacious acceptance to those symptoms we cannot change.

• Letting go of the past so that we may be more fully present.

• Taking refuge in the awareness of consciousness itself, in which experience manifests.

• Creating positive intentions, healing prescriptions and affirmations for the future.

• Opening to the question, "What is the healing this symptom needs?" rather than meeting our symptoms with judgment, fear and anger.

• Recognizing the universal in our symptoms. Recognizing that we are not separate from one another, that others also suffer the same symptoms.

• Recognizing that we are more than our symptoms, which enlarges the context in which our symptoms occur.

THE ROLE OF DIRECTED ATTENTION AND INTENTION IN THE TREATMENT PROCESS

Awareness is a function of consciousness. It is always present, all-pervasive and illuminating everything. Awareness, like consciousness, is open, alert, intelligent, beyond duality and thus unaffected by our conditioning or any of our symptoms.

Unlike awareness, attention is a function of the egoic mind. What any of us is aware of at any one time depends upon where we direct our attention. Our attention may be on our thoughts; we may be thinking about something in the past or something in the future. Our attention may be on the body, on how it is feeling, on its aches and pains. Our attention may be on our mood or emotional state. Attention constantly shifts and changes and although we can direct it, it is often drawn to some area of focus without our explicit direction.

Harnessing the ability to direct attention is often the first step toward healing. Directing attention toward a description of our symptoms, their origin and how we experience them in the mind and body leads to greater self-understanding. Although some people are more adept in their ability to perceive and describe their symptoms than others, most people can learn to enhance this ability and direct it toward healing.

During a Reiki treatment the therapist can guide the client as to how to direct her attention, and how to identify, select and investigate a symptom. For example, placing her attention on the experience of anxiety, instead of distracting from it, can yield helpful information in treating the anxiety.

Learning to direct attention can contribute to healing in the following ways:

- Bringing systematic attention to the body increases

the client's ability to abide with the body in presence.

•   Bringing systematic attention to the body helps to develop a fuller picture of the embodied symptom.

•   Feeling into the energy field of the inner body promotes grounding and anchoring in the body.

•   Connecting with the flow of Reiki and directing Reiki into areas of imbalance help treat these areas: "Where thought goes, energy flows."

•   Directing attention toward mental, emotional, physical, relational and spiritual blockages helps in releasing those blockages.

•   Sending positive healing emotions and intentions to the mind and body helps the client to focus on what needs healing.

The efficacy of using directed attention is affected by the kind of intention the client holds toward her symptoms. In other words, the quality of the attention she gives a symptom is determined by her intention. Whereas resisting a symptom often intensifies it, turning toward it often calms it. When we relate to a symptom with fear, anger, judgment or avoidance, the symptom tends to entrench itself and often intensifies. If the symptom is forced to go "underground" for a while, it will likely reemerge even stronger and more intractable.

On the other hand, when we make the effort to turn our attention *toward* a symptom, to enter into it mindfully and to soften around it, a spaciousness opens up which makes treating the symptom more workable. Mindfully turning toward a symptom alters our relationship to it. Instead of relating from it, we are now relating to it. From this perspective we are relating to the symptom as an "other," as one in need of our care and heartfelt compassion.

Reiki is responsive to positive intention, as it works for the highest good. When the therapist and client align their positive intention with the Reiki energy during a treatment, they are maximizing the healing potential. Using positive intention with a symptom and sending kindness to it facilitates its healing and transformation.

The following are ways to involve intention in the Four Therapeutic Tasks:

• While working with the therapeutic task of Practicing Presence, hold the intention to be present with openhearted attention. Hold the intention to quiet the mind, calm the body, and open the heart. Hold the intentions to connect with the flow of Reiki and to rest in acceptance and non-judgmental awareness. Hold the intention to meet an unchangeable symptom with greater acceptance in the present.

• While working with the therapeutic task of Exploring the Body-Mind, hold the intention to receive clarity and insight into the nature of a symptom. Hold the intention to uncover its "origin" and its interconnecting parts.

• While working with the therapeutic task of Releasing and Clearing Energy Blocks, hold the intention to let go of unreleased emotional pain and held trauma energy.

Hold the intention to let go of self-limiting thoughts, beliefs and judgments. Hold the intention to ease acute and chronic pain.

• While working with the therapeutic task of Installing Corrective Experience, hold a belief in your healing potential and your ability to reduce symptoms. Hold the intention to cultivate hope and optimism in the present and for the future.

BREATH WORK AS A HOLISTIC TOOL

I use breath work as a holistic tool to support and enhance all four of the therapeutic tasks. Breath work helps to focus awareness and relax the body. Following the breath while receiving Reiki helps to quiet the mind and soothe mental agitation, and it allows clients to be more present and grounded. Breathing "into and out of" areas of pain and energy blockage is useful for exploring those areas of holding and for releasing any tension that is found there. There are also methods for using the breath to send Reiki into the body and H.E.F., to strengthen and intensify the flow of Ki.

Abdominal Breathing

Have your client slowly inhale for three to five seconds and expand her belly like a balloon. Instruct her to hold her breath for several seconds, then gently release. Having the client practice abdominal breathing while receiving Reiki is an excellent method for calming the body and releasing strong emotion. This is similar to a Japanese Reiki breathing exercise called *Joshin Kokyuu-Ho*, which translates as "breathing exercise to purify the spirit" (Lübeck, Petter & Rand, 2001, p. 158).

As your client inhales through her nose, have her imagine that she is pulling Reiki energy into her body through the crown chakra, while you hold your hands on the crown of her head. Along with her breath, have her pull the energy down into her tanden or sacral chakra. Instruct her to hold the breath and the Reiki energy there for a few seconds without straining herself. Ask her to visualize the Reiki filling her entire body, expanding from her center out through her arms and legs to the tips of her fingers and toes. Finally, have her exhale through her mouth and imagine the Reiki flowing out of her hands and feet.

Koki-Ho

Koki-Ho is a Reiki Level Two technique that utilizes the breath to send Reiki into the body of the client with whom you are working. Inhale and pull the breath down to your tanden or sacral chakra. While holding the breath there, draw the power symbol on the roof of your mouth with your tongue, or visualize it there. Then exhale and breathe the power symbol onto the client's body area or chakra being treated. You can use this method with other Reiki symbols and you can use this with the physical body, with the client's energy field and with photographs when sending distance Reiki (Lübeck, Petter & Rand, 2001).

Ekhart Tolle (2005) discusses using breath work with

any compulsive behavior pattern like smoking, drinking or over-eating. Tolle (2005) writes:

> When you notice the compulsive need arising in you, stop and take three conscious breaths. This generates awareness. Then for a few minutes be aware of the compulsive urge itself as an energy field inside you. Consciously feel that need to physically or mentally ingest or consume a certain substance or the desire to act out some form of compulsive behavior. Then take a few more conscious breaths. After that you may find that the compulsive urge has disappeared – for the time being. Or you may find that it still overpowers you, and you cannot help but indulge or act it out again. Don't make it a problem. Make the addiction part of your awareness practice in the way described above. As awareness grows, addictive patterns will weaken and eventually dissolve. (p. 247)

IMAGERY AND VISUALIZATION

The body communicates with us through the language of imagery, visualizations and symbols. This is evident in the rich images and symbols expressed in daydreams and the dream state, and in instances of creativity such as when your body tells you it is hungry by bringing to mind pictures of your favorite foods when you weren't even thinking about eating. Our emotional life and the experiences we have are stored in images and symbols that are often more expressive than words alone (e.g., "I was so restless, I felt like a caged animal").

Imagery and visualization can help the practitioner and client tune into what is happening in the body-mind and access symptoms that are stored there. In conjunction with Reiki, images and visualizations are useful with all four of the therapeutic tasks. They are a creative way to promote relaxation, decrease stress and negative emotional states, and ease physical pain. They are descriptive and yield a richer, fuller picture of our symptoms. They are useful allies in releasing and letting go, and in helping encode new information in the body-mind. For many clients, using imagery and visualization serves to focus their awareness and attention and engage their participation in the treatment process.

In their book *Rituals of Healing*, Jeanne Achterberg, Barbara Dossey and Leslie Kolkmeier (1994) present an excellent overview of how to use visualization and imagery for health and wellness. They describe four different types of imagery: *receptive*, *active*, *process* and *end state*.

Receptive imagery consists of images that "flow through or 'bubble' up into the conscious mind – one doesn't deliberately create these images. Receptive imagery is especially provocative and creative right before dropping off to sleep or upon awakening" (Achterberg, Dossey & Kolkmeier, 1994, p. 38). Reiki often induces a calm, open and relaxed state, which helps clients receive receptive images. While using the techniques for Practicing Presence and Exploring the Body-Mind, the therapist can encourage the client to focus his attention on a symptomatic area inside the body. The therapist might say, "Allow your mind to move into that area and picture what's happening there." The receptive images that come to mind help the client to describe and experience his symptoms and to discover information helpful to the treatment.

Active imagery, according to Achterberg, Dossey and Kolkmeier (1994), is "imagery that you consciously and deliberately construct. You take charge of your thoughts, consciously choosing images that are important to your well-being" (p. 39). Active imagery uses the client's personal symbology – images and symbols that have meaning and relevance to her. For example, tightness in the neck might be seen as a vise clamping down on a muscle by one person and as a stretched rubber band by another. Active imagery can be particularly useful when a client harnesses the power of a personal symbol, such as healing light, to release the charge underlying a symptom.

Process imagery is "imaging step-by-step toward the goal one wishes to achieve. . . For physical healing, this means imaging the detailed action of inner healing, such as the immune system's functions, as well as how any treatment is working" (Achterberg, Dossey & Kolkmeier, 1994, p. 41). For emotional healing, process imagery can be helpful in treating unresolved traumatic incidents, phobias or fear-producing situations. As in the use of traditional desensitization techniques, have your client develop a hierarchy of scenes, from the least to the most stressful, leading up to the traumatic incident or fear-producing situation. Then, starting with the least stressful image, use Reiki with the Practicing Presence and Releasing and Clearing techniques to gradually reduce anxiety by releasing the emotional charge underlying these scenes.

If your client experiences fear-producing thoughts during a visualization, encourage him to allow these thoughts to be present without engaging in or being controlled by them. You can encourage him to focus his attention on his breathing as a way to assist in grounding. Remind him that the focus of the exercise is to be present with the emotion and allow it to fade. When your client's anxiety level has diminished and he is sufficiently comfortable with the visualization, he can then move to the next stressful image and work with it. Take as many sessions as needed to work with each scene in the hierarchy.

End state imagery involves picturing the final healed state of an injury, phobia or trauma, or visualizing a desired goal. End state imagery usually comes at the end of process imaging, but if you don't know how the healing is supposed to take place then you can just picture the final desired result. For example, imagining a broken bone or injured body part in its completely healed state, or a desired behavior or emotional state achieved, can be effective end state imagery.

For most healing visualizations it is important to rely upon a source of power as an aid to healing (Thondup, 1996). A source of power is a tool that can awaken the energy and the wisdom within us for healing. Tulku Thondup (1996) writes that it could be "any positive form, nature, essence or force," such as the image or presence of a spiritual divinity, or it could be a force in nature such as the sun, moon, sky, ocean, river, forest, mountain, light or sound (p. 93). This could include "any aspect of energy that one finds inspiring and healing" (Thondup, 1996, p. 93). Healing light coming from a power source is a commonly used image, as it has many uses and can be directed at darkness, coldness, pain, disease, injury, sorrow or disharmony in the body or mind.

According to Achterberg, Dossey and Kolkmeier (1994), there are several steps involved in preparing and using a visual healing ritual:

1. Define the problem, injury or goal to treat.

2. Develop the healing images and resources you plan to use to treat the problem. If you are using process imagery, define the stages or steps to follow.

3. Define the optimal end result and what that would look like. Finish with visualizations of the healed state of being.

Thondup (1996) states, "The most important point in visualizing is to call up the positive image with warmth and whole-heartedness" (p. 45). The key is to feel the presence of what you are imagining. Thondup (1996) continues, "Your visualization doesn't need to be elaborate or detailed; the clarity and stability of your mental images are what matters" (p. 45).

Examples of Therapeutic Images and Visualizations

• A client suffering from a disease focused her inner vision on the afflicted organ system. She allowed images and impressions to form and described what she was seeing. Then, she envisioned healing light coming from a particular saint to whom she had prayed all of her life. She then pictured this saint sending this light into her body as she received Reiki.

• When a client is feeling the presence of a troubling emotion, such as sadness, fear, worry or anger, have the client picture this emotion as a dark cloud or a mist within or throughout her body. Have the client stay with this experience and allow herself to fully feel it. Then guide her to imagine and feel the Reiki energy flowing into and slowly dispelling this cloud, replacing it with white, healing light.

• Sui (2000) discusses several visualization techniques for clearing negative thoughts and feelings, depressing or fearful thoughts and traumatic memory. To do this, have your client externalize the negative thought, memory or feeling by visualizing a large white board in front of his eyes and then projecting these negative thoughts and feelings onto this board. Next, the client can dissolve these images by erasing them from the board with an energetic eraser and positive intention. Another way the client can externalize and dissolve negative thoughts is to visualize a boiling cauldron into which he can throw all the thoughts. Alternatively, he can transmute negative thoughts by imagining throwing them into a fire (Sui, 2000, p. 99).

• One client was feeling particularly anxious about an upcoming talk she had to give to a rather large audience. We constructed a hierarchy of three scenes from the least to the most anxiety-provoking. First, she pictured herself driving in her car on the way to the talk. Then she pictured herself sitting on the panel in front of the audience waiting to speak, and finally she pictured herself actually giving the talk.

While giving her Reiki, I had her visualize herself driving to the talk and encouraged her to let herself feel the anxiety welling up in her. I encouraged her to breathe in and out of the anxiety, to pay attention to where she felt it in her body and to identify any fear-producing thoughts that were arising, but not to engage with them. She noticed that when she allowed the anxiety to exist and practiced being present with it, it began to subside. Over the next several sessions we worked similarly with the other two scenes until they also felt less emotionally charged and more manageable. This experience not only decreased her anxiety but increased her confidence in her ability to handle the talk.

• Have your client picture the steps involved in the attainment of a goal and see himself successfully accomplishing each step. Then guide him to visualize himself reaching the goal. This is a helpful approach when working with addictions. Bill was in AA and working at developing a comfortable sobriety, but he had frequent relapses. He sought Reiki as an adjunctive approach to see if it could help. Bill and I developed a series of images that would support his recovery, which we installed during Reiki sessions using the Sei He Ki technique (as described in Chapter 5).

First, Bill pictured successful ways he had coped with life's stresses before he had ever begun drinking. He remembered what it was like to be free of addiction. He pictured the successful avoidance of alcohol at his most vulnerable time of day. Next, he pictured calling program friends and reaching out to others when he had the urge to drink. Then, he pictured himself exercising and working out when he felt stressed. Finally, he pictured himself living a healthy lifestyle free from alcohol.

• Debby had frequent tension headaches in response to stress. She had seen her doctor, who recommended that she learn meditation or relaxation training. She called me to try Reiki, which we began doing on a weekly basis. She responded well to the Reiki and I attuned her to it so that she could use it on herself between sessions. One week she came in with a particularly bad headache and we decided to try a guided visualization to explore and release the headache while I gave her Reiki.

I took my lead from Debby and used the images she produced as she narrated our journey. First, she had us shrink in size so we could climb into her ear. Once in the ear canal, we found steps going up to a platform, looking out over the brain and the inside of her head. We circled the platform, looking for the area of tension, which we found in the musculature at the base of the inside of her skull. Debby saw fiery red, throbbing muscular bands coming up from the neck and connecting to the base of the brain.

I asked her how she thought we should approach the problem and she suggested we look through the backpack she had brought to see if there was anything useful in it. As she went through the backpack, she found a can of aerosol spray labeled "Dissolve Away" and decided to spray this on the inflamed muscles. After a bit, the muscles began to relax and turn back to a normal shade of red and she felt her headache beginning to ease. We decided to pack up, retrace our steps and return "home." This guided visualization took about twenty minutes and then I continued to give her Reiki until the end of the session. By that time her headache was completely gone.

ORGANIZATION OF TREATMENT TECHNIQUES

Throughout the remainder of this book, examples of techniques for Practicing Presence, Exploring the Body-Mind, Releasing and Clearing Energy Blocks, and Installing Corrective Experience are organized and presented under chapters focused on the physical body, the mind, emotion, the heart, held energy of relationship trauma, and treatment templates for psychological issues. This organization is problem-focused and you might find it useful to read through all of the techniques sequentially, or you can move directly to one of the above chapters and find specific Reiki techniques for working with a presenting problem. The Index of Techniques also presents a list of all techniques organized by the Four Therapeutic Tasks.

As you read through the various techniques, you will

notice a repetition of core concepts. Hopefully this repetition will help to familiarize you with these concepts and make it easier for you to find creative ways to apply them. It is important to note that these techniques are not intended as a one-time, "quick fix" solution to treating psychological symptoms. They typically need to be repeated and incorporated into an ongoing treatment process.

The physical body is the "ground" of the H.E.F., storing and carrying the effects and symptoms of unresolved mental, emotional and relational trauma and stress.

Chapter 4

Working with the Physical Body

As the vehicle of the H.E.F. and the repository of its experiences, the physical body carries and reflects the effects and symptoms of unresolved and unreleased mental, emotional and relational trauma and chronic stress. Reiki is an effective method for bringing the body into a relaxed state and for reducing the stress that the body carries, and at times I use Reiki for this purpose alone. However, Reiki also brings awareness to the ways our symptoms are stored, manifest and are expressing in the body.

When we are centered in the egoic mind, our thoughts are generally focused on the past or the future and rarely on the present. When we are centered in the body, we can recognize that the mind is too occupied to be present. It is a paradox that the body holds the effects of the past and at the same time lives in the present, but it is only in the present that we can access our body's symptoms and work to heal them. This shift in perspective enables us to become grounded in the body, and from there to observe and modify the mind's conditioning.

Because the body carries the rich world of our mental, emotional, relational, and spiritual experiences, there is wisdom there from which we can draw. When we establish a connection to the body in the present, we can access this experience and bring it to bear on the symptoms we are having. The more present we are in the physical body, the more workable our problems become.

Body-Mind Disconnect

Growing up in Western culture, which places such high value on honing the mind and the intellect, it is common to develop symptoms that express a disconnection between the mind and the body. This disconnection occurs when the mind overrides, denies, ignores or contradicts messages coming from the body and the body's experience. When the mind ignores the body's reactions to traumatic events, stress or negative conditioning, these reactions become repressed and shut away from the mind's awareness. The result is that the body can be expressing emotional and physical symptoms that the mind doesn't register or understand.

The following are common reasons people suffer from body-mind disconnection:

• They may have grown up in a family or culture that devalued the importance of the body or stressed the development of intellect at the expense of the body.

• They may be trying to actively distance themselves from the body due to feelings of shame or embarrassment about how it looks, or their perception of its inadequacies.

• They may feel discouraged and depressed by limitations imposed upon the body due to aging, illness, accident or injury.

• They may feel anger toward the body for causing them physical pain or for having suffered an injury that impairs the body's ability to function. Fear of contracting a chronic and perhaps fatal illness or living in fear that a present illness will worsen pits people against the body as if it were an enemy.

• They may feel fatigued, anxious, and depressed in response to living with bodily symptoms like chronic pain, actively attempting to tune it out or becoming self-medicating to deal with the physical and emotional discomfort they are experiencing. Some ignore their discomfort and push themselves to the point that they experience physical or emotional symptoms, aversive behavior patterns or stress reactions.

• They may have experienced a trauma or stress too great to be integrated. In this case, the mind dissociates from the body and the symptoms of the trauma or stress become embodied (stored in the body). Over time, a variety of symptoms can emerge including emotional flooding, numbing, or conscious or unconscious behavioral re-enactments of the original trauma or stress.

Under any of these circumstances, people have significant difficulty connecting with their bodies and attuning to the messages their bodies are expressing. The result of this conditioning and these emotional reactions is that we learn to distance and disconnect ourselves from the body and perhaps even come to fear it. Tuning out and turning away from our bodily symptoms intensifies them, leaving us feeling fragmented and ungrounded and blocking us from accessing our healing potential.

Techniques for Practicing Presence and Exploring the Body-Mind are directed toward helping clients reconnect with their bodies and develop a fuller picture of how their psychological symptoms are manifesting in the body. Being connected with the body means being able to open and attune to the ongoing stream of energy, information, emotion, physical sensation, thought, and intuition that is always flowing throughout the body and the H.E.F.

Reiki energy helps the client tune into the body, listen to it, explore the symptoms it is expressing and carefully retrieve the stored memory and emotion it is carrying. Learning to attend to this flow of information with an attitude of openness and self-compassion sets the stage for greater healing. Once this has been accomplished, installing corrective affirmations can aid in maintaining this reconnection to the body, and in learning to relax and live in it more comfortably.

Shainberg (2000) writes, "Giving the experiences we have inside a space to exist and paying attention to them and accepting them is coming to life and healing into being ourselves" (p. 26). Using Reiki and being present with our internal experience in a nonjudgmental and compassionate way can be transformational.

I was working with a woman with a diagnosis of ADD who was distractible, unfocused and disconnected from her body. As she began to focus on and attend to bodily feelings and sensations, the Reiki brought out trauma memories that psychotherapy was able to help her resolve over time.

While giving Reiki to a woman who hadn't gotten her period in two years, she had the experience that her body was "frozen." As Reiki helped her to relax and to "thaw," she began to reconnect to her body and to access body memories that were important for her healing process.

A woman came into therapy with the complaint that she felt dissociated and numb much of the time. As the Reiki treatment helped her develop the capacity to stay present in her body, it also brought out aches and pains that her dissociation had kept her from feeling. These aches and pains were associated with repressed memories and feelings about her childhood, and Reiki and therapy helped her to process them.

A man who grew up in a violent and unsafe home felt trapped in an unsafe body that he feared could become injured or ill at any time. Several months of

Reiki treatment and psychotherapy with a focus on Practicing Presence exercises increased his sense of bodily safety and comfort, along with his self-confidence.

Whenever Janet was confronted by something she didn't want to do, she felt sick to her stomach, panicky, and trapped, and wanted to run away. But she had learned to ignore these symptoms and comply with what she felt she had to do. Her mind told her to distrust her own judgment, that others knew her needs better than she knew her own, and that she had to do what others asked in order to get approval and feel good about herself.

Over the course of time Janet's physical and emotional symptoms worsened and prompted her to seek help. Reiki treatments made her aware of this body-mind split and the symptoms it was creating. While I gave Reiki, we explored the childhood experiences and conditioning that led to her difficulties. We created corrective experiences and affirmations that supported her needs and she put these into practice in her relationships with others.

Reiki and the State of Presence

My daughter Sarah, a long-time Reiki practitioner, was receiving a therapeutic massage when she felt herself entering into a familiar altered state of sensation. "Oh," she thought to herself, "I know this feeling – it feels like Reiki." When she mentioned this to the massage therapist, the therapist smiled and revealed that she was a Reiki Master and that Reiki naturally flowed through her hands during a treatment. Because it evoked a calming state of presence within Sarah, she immediately recognized that she was receiving Reiki as well as a massage.

When you receive Reiki, you will notice that it quiets the mind, calms the body and opens the heart, all effects of coming into conscious and sensory contact with the field of Ki, consciousness itself. This field is still, alert, open, intelligent, and beyond the duality of the egoic mind. Consciousness is always present but we are not always aware of it or receptive to it because we are caught in ego, in the conditioned mind.

When we are in conscious contact with this field we are said to be in presence. In presence, we are better able to focus and direct our attention, to see more deeply into a problem, to experience insight, and to access the body's healing potential so that symptoms can transform. In presence, we notice that our focal vision softens and our peripheral vision sharpens as our sense perceptions open and become clearer. Presence is the space in which perceiving happens; we perceive the mind thinking, we perceive our emotions expressing, and we perceive the body and the changing stream of bodily sensations.

Try this exercise with your client to discover Reiki's effectiveness in putting her into conscious contact with presence. Prior to the start of receiving Reiki, have your client sit or lie down with her arms by her sides and her hands off the body. Have her focus her attention on some object in the room, following her breath or feeling sensations in the body. Ask her to try and relax and notice her present moment experience just as it is. After two to three minutes, begin giving your client Reiki. You might try placing your hands on the crown of her head, on the back of her head or on her heart and solar plexus chakras.

Ask her to notice how Reiki begins to affect her. Have her notice how it brings her attention into the present and deepens her experience. Reiki brings us into the body and connects us with an underlying feeling of peace, a comforting silence. Your client may feel an inner spaciousness opening, a feeling of expansiveness as if her awareness is extending outside of her physical body and into the field around her. She might detect a feeling of aliveness in her body and/or a feeling of energy flow, a mild current flowing down the body and out the hands and feet. Many people experience an increase in sense perception accompanied by a decrease in thinking. As your client moves into an energetically open and receptive mode, she is in a better position to release or remove energy blockages and reduce psychological symptoms.

An Exercise for Noticing, Allowing, Opening and Relaxing (NAOR)

While giving the client Reiki, have him focus on the presenting problem or primary symptom. Instruct him to bring his attention to the present and *notice* any bodily sensations, images, thoughts or emotions that arise. Instruct him to experience these symptoms as fully as he can while *allowing* these symptoms to be just as they are. As the client *opens* to his symptoms, have him pay attention to any resistance that arises and try to let it go. Encourage him to breathe slowly, deeply and evenly and to *relax* around his symptoms.

This exercise teaches clients to open to their symptoms, explore them more fully, decrease the fear they have about them, and increase their insight and sense of control over them. Paradoxically, turning toward our symptoms and embracing them can help to diminish their perceived power over us, thereby transforming them.

CASE EXAMPLE

Sam was seeking help with chronic fatigue, excessive anxiety and worry. He explained that he never knew when the anxiety would hit him or how long it would last. His approach to dealing with these attacks was to try to push them away and distract himself from them. Sam worried that these anxiety attacks were an indicator that he had a serious undiagnosed mental or physical illness that was getting worse. We began using the NAOR exercise to see if this could help Sam manage his anxiety better.

At first this was a difficult exercise for Sam to try,

as he feared that concentrating on his anxiety would only make it worse. After several weeks of working with this exercise Sam was better able to focus on, tolerate and describe his symptoms. As Sam directed attention to his anxiety he became aware of muscular tension in his chest, arms, neck, and head. He was aware of fleeting, worrisome thoughts about the upcoming week and he noticed that these thoughts increased his anxiety. He pictured these thoughts as a ball of worry in his solar plexus.

As he noticed these things, he felt his body relax and he became aware of a background sensation of fatigue. He had the insight that this fatigue was his body's response to the effort it took to live in a state of chronic tension and worry. Sam recognized that he lived largely in one of these two states, either chronic anxiety and worry or chronic fatigue. The focus on body process was the beginning of helping Sam to work on his problem with anxiety.

Although Sam was not trying to do anything with his anxiety except to focus on it, describe it and be present with it, he developed more insight into the nature of it, and to other related symptoms he was experiencing. As this process occurred, his body began to relax and his anxiety eased. Sam found the NAOR exercise to be a useful self-help tool in developing tolerance and understanding around his symptoms.

Body Scan

The body scan is a good method to use for detecting where mental, emotional and relational issues have taken up residence in the body. By bringing systematic attention to the body we can identify and explore areas of imbalance, tension, pain or emotional holding. The body scan also gives clients practice in coming home to the body and developing a greater level of comfort with being in the body.

Have the client start at the top of her head and using her inner vision as a "search light," scan the inside of her body looking or feeling for areas of imbalance such as emotional holding and held trauma energy. Such imbalance may be "seen" as sensation with a certain shape to it, or "felt" as an area of coldness, restricted energy flow, heat, tingling or pain. When your client locates an area of imbalance, treat it with Reiki.

CASE EXAMPLE

Rick presented with problems of emotional pain and grief, as well as a heart condition. We used the body scan to locate where in the body he stored grief. He intuitively "saw" grey coloration around his heart and as I gave him Reiki, he watched this grey begin to move out. This movement brought up mental and emotional issues related to his grief. We used the body scan, Reiki, and talk therapy for a

> number of sessions to help him process his deeper grief.

Field Scan

The Field Scan is a method to assess body, mind and emotion. Have your client focus his attention on the present and allow his awareness to move into the space of the heart center. From there, have him observe the mind and describe the state of the mind. Now have him look at his emotionality and describe his emotional state. Finally, have him look at the body, scan the body and describe what he is feeling. Does he notice any areas of held tension, sensation or pain? What mental, emotional or physical issues are associated with these symptoms? You can work with a combination of Reiki and talk therapy to help him sort through and process what comes up.

Byosen

Byosen is a Japanese word that translates to mean "toxic lump," "energy block" or "meridian imbalance," a condition in which the fluids, flows and energy of the body are disrupted and lead to a poor internal environment in the body and energy field (Yamaguchi, 2007). Energy blockages are not necessarily the cause of physical, emotional or mental disorders, but according to Joyce Hawkes (2006), a biophysicist and energy healer, energy blockages and obstructions prevent healing from occurring. In her book

Cell-Level Healing, she states that vibrant health is associated with the robust flow of Ki, whereas obstructed flow is associated with ill health: "A natural return to unobstructed flow of [Ki] occurs when blockages are removed, allowing body, mind, and spirit to be open and clear" (Hawkes, 2006, p. 35).

As discussed in Chapter 1, energy blockages can develop on any level of the human energy field and subsequently create blockages on other levels.

• Physical blockages may result from the presence of toxins, physical illness, disease, injury or side effects of surgery.

• Emotional blockages may result from stress, unresolved trauma, negative conditioning or unreleased emotional pain.

• Mental blockages may be created by self-limiting and self-defeating negative beliefs and constructs, compulsive thinking, worry and rumination.

• Spiritual blockages may be created by a restricted or intolerant upbringing, forced religiosity or an environment where one is not allowed to question, learn and think for oneself. They are expressed in an inability to feel inner peace, compassion, joy of life or connection with a spiritual core, as well as an inability to see oneself as part of a greater whole.

In most cases physical illness begins with *byosen* in the kidney region. Then toxins migrate to the region between the shoulder blades, the shoulders, armpits, neck and all of the joints in the body (Yamaguchi, 2007). Mental, emotional and spiritual *byosen* may be scattered throughout the body but often collect in energy centers and chakras that process the particular issues with which the client is struggling. (Refer to the discussion of the chakras in Chapter 1 for further information.)

Reiki is a particular frequency of Ki that has the capacity to detect the presence of energy blocks (*byosen*) and to help the body clear and release them. According to Tadao Yamaguchi (2007) in his book *Light on the Origins of Reiki*, Chujiro Hayashi, one of Usui's students, taught his own students that after receiving attunement to Reiki they would be able to feel unique sensations in their hands when they laid them on the part of the body that has *byosen*.

Dr. Hayashi taught his students that there are five levels of sensation in the practitioner's hands, explained by Yamaguchi (2007) as follows:

> 1. *On-Netsu (Warmth)*: When your hands are placed on a stiff part of a receiver's body you will sense warmth (1ˢᵗ level), which is slightly higher than the usual body temperature.
>
> 2. *Atsui-On-Netsu (Intense Heat)*: It will be followed by more intense heat (2ⁿᵈ level).
>
> 3. *Piri-Piri Kan (Tingling Sensation)*: If the stiffness in the body is even more serious your hands will have a tingling sensation in the palms or fingertips. Some people describe this as "numbness" and others as "electric vibration."

4. *Hibiki (Throbbing Sensation)*: *Hibiki* is a pulse-like sensation in your hands, which indicates that you can actually feel the Reiki stimulating blood vessels, causing them to expand and contract. At this time the blood circulation is activated and the blood begins to flow more smoothly.

5. *Itami (Pain)*: *Itami* means a pain, which tells you that the receiver's *Byosen* is quite serious. If the problem is more serious, your hands will feel more painful. Pain can move from your palm to the back of your hand, to your wrist and gradually to around the elbow area. Sometimes it stops there and at other times it may move up to your shoulder. After the pain eases, the tingling sensation you felt also simultaneously decreases. When they experience this pain some people become worried about being affected by negative energy from the receiver, but this is not possible so do not worry unnecessarily. Taking your hands off the receiver can easily relieve the pain although occasionally it still continues for a while. (p. 74)

When you find a strong area of *byosen*, concentrate there before moving on to another location. You will recognize when the *byosen* is releasing as the sensations in your hands will balance out and ease.

Byosen Scanning

Byosen scanning is a technique Usui taught in his Reiki classes (Lübeck, Petter & Rand, 2001). This technique is a useful tool for identifying areas of energy blockage in the client's body and energy field. To perform *byosen* scanning on your client, put your hands together in a prayer position in front of your heart and ask for connection to your Reiki guides. Bring your hands up to your third eye and ask for guidance about where in the body this client needs healing. You may get a fleeting image or hear the name of an energy center needing treatment, or you may just feel drawn to work on a certain part of the body. Trust your intuition, however subtle, and begin treatment there. Apply Reiki to this area for as long as you feel necessary or until the *byosen* sensations in your hands have calmed down. Follow your intuition as to where to work next.

In the event that you do not receive guidance or intuition as to where to start the treatment, you can scan the client's energy field with your hands. Starting above the client's crown, and with your palms facing the client's body, slowly scan the field above the client's body while moving toward the feet. Sense for areas of heat, cold or tingling; these are the areas in need of treatment. Listen to your intuition and trust your impressions.

In my opinion, following the standard hand positions format is also a form of *byosen* scanning because your hands are systematically moving down the body and will detect *byosen* as you go. When you detect an energy blockage, continue with Reiki on this placement until the *byosen* is cleared and then move on.

Exploration and Release

Mind and emotion exist in every cell of the body, which means that the unreleased and unresolved effects of traumatic experience may be lodged anywhere in the body and can communicate with other body areas. Reiki can be used to investigate areas of unreleased trauma, bring out their meaning and assist in their release. When you find an area of tension, pain or held energy in a client, give Reiki to it while instructing the client to breathe deeply, slowly and evenly. Have the client hold an attitude of relaxed attention and acceptance while he allows his intuition to bring to mind any thoughts, images, memories or feelings being held in this part of the body.

If there is not an immediately obvious area of pain or tension, you can use Reiki to explore deeper-held issues. For example, you could try giving Reiki to the client while asking him to bring his mind back to a time when he felt a certain feeling (e.g., loneliness), or to a traumatic incident he experienced. Ask the client where in the body he feels the effects of these memories, and give Reiki to this area.

You could also ask the client to tell you the thoughts he has about himself as a child, while giving Reiki to the back of his head. What adjectives would he use to describe himself when he was young? Ask the client to notice the feelings these adjectives cause and let these feelings arise as best they can, while he remains present with them. Have him notice where in the body these thoughts and feelings are stored. Where does he have sensation while doing this exercise? You can then move your hands to the identified areas and give Reiki. If it is useful, you can formulate a corrective message to place in the area(s), using the power symbol to install this message.

Releasing Body Memory

Areas of coldness in the client's energy field may indicate areas of held trauma energy, and a technique discussed by Julie Motz (1998) may be useful in exploring this. This technique is called Releasing Body Memory, or held trauma energy, and is detailed in her book *Hands of Life*. When you find an area of coldness in the client's energy field indicating an energy deficiency, ask your client to bring her awareness to that area of the body and imagine being that body part. Have the client speak about her impressions of what might be held or stored there as you give Reiki to that area.

To end the treatment, tell the client that you are now going to raise your hands from that body part and draw the imbalance out. Imagine using Reiki to pull out the trauma energy and "clean" out the area, and visualize sending the removed energy into the light to be healed. This is similar to the aura clearing technique discussed in detail in Chapter 8. Generally, this technique has a calming effect, but at times it may generate a stronger emotional release so you need to be prepared for this possibility (Motz, 1998).

CASE EXAMPLE

I had a client who felt an area of coldness on her upper chest at the base of her throat. As she focused her attention there, she felt anxious and had a fear of suffocating. As I gave her Reiki and gently pulled at this area, she suddenly sat up with a startled reaction and was flooded with memories of being thrown into a pool and almost drowning as a child. We spent several sessions processing and releasing these memories while treating her with Reiki.

Sweeping

Sui (1990) describes a technique called sweeping that is useful for treating areas of energy congestion, depletion or imbalance, and which helps clear negative elements that are lodged in the client's energy field. Sweeping involves repeatedly passing your hands over, through and around either generalized or localized areas of the client's H.E.F. For example, if the client is feeling anxiety in the area of her solar plexus, sweep your hands over this area twenty-five to thirty times and then apply Reiki.

Balancing and Vitalizing Chakras

When you have detected a mental, emotional or physical energy imbalance in the client's H.E.F., you can treat this obstruction by working on the corresponding chakra. First, clear the energy block with Reiki and/or one of the clearing techniques discussed in this book, such as sweeping (see the Index of Techniques for a full list of clearing and releasing exercises). Then vitalize the chakra with Reiki while both you and the client visualize the color of the chakra growing steadily stronger and brighter. You may want to follow this step by installing a corrective message into the chakra to assist in rebalancing it, and then using the power symbol to seal it in. This process is detailed in the following section.

Installing Corrective Messages in Chakras

As discussed in Chapter 1, certain traumas and abuses in a person's life cause chakra imbalance in either excessive or deficient directions. When you find imbalance in a particular chakra, you can install a healing or corrective message to help rebalance it. Simply apply Reiki to that chakra while both you and the client hold and repeat to yourselves the corrective message.

The following examples are taken directly from *Eastern Body, Western Mind*, by Judith (2004):

> **1ˢᵗ chakra** – the right to be here and to have:
> "It is safe for me to be here."
> "The earth supports me and meets my needs."
> "I love my body and trust its wisdom." (p. 53)
>
> **2ⁿᵈ chakra** – the right to feel and have pleasure:
> "I deserve pleasure in my life."
> "I absorb information from my feelings."
> "I embrace and celebrate my sexuality." (p. 105)
>
> **3ʳᵈ chakra** – the right to act and be an individual:
> "I honor the power within me."
> "I accomplish tasks easily and effortlessly."

"I can do whatever I will to do." (p. 167)

4th chakra – the right to love and to be loved:
"I am worthy of love."
"I am loving to myself and others."
"There is an infinite supply of love."
"I live in balance with others." (p. 223)

5th chakra – the right to speak and to be heard:
"I hear and speak the truth."
"I express myself with clear intent."
"Creativity flows in and through me."
"My voice is necessary." (p. 287)

6th chakra – the right to see:
"I see all things in clarity."
"I am open to the wisdom within."
"I can manifest my vision." (p. 339)

7th chakra – the right to know and to learn:
"Divinity resides within."
"I am open to new ideas."
"Information I need comes to me."
"I am guided by higher power."
"I am guided by inner wisdom." (p. 391)

Kekko Massage (Ketseuki Kokan Ho)

Kekko Massage was one of the main Reiki Level Two techniques taught by Dr. Hayasho (Petter, Yamaguchi &

Hayashi, 2003). Kekko Massage is an effective treatment for a wide variety of problems because it stimulates blood circulation, strengthens the flow of Ki and promotes the release of toxins. Dr. Hayashi recommended using Kekko at the end of a Reiki treatment.

This practice might be out of your or your client's comfort zone, but I am including Kekko Massage in this book because I believe it will appeal to counseling body-workers and massage therapists who incorporate Reiki in their work.

To practice Kekko Massage, have the client lay face-down on the Reiki table and follow these steps outlined by Yamaguchi (2007):

1.   Find the indentations located on either side of the neck at the base of the skull.

2.   Place the thumb and index finger of one hand in the indentations and draw parallel power symbols there (this sends intensified Reiki into the head).

3.   Place the index and middle finger of one hand on either side of the client's spine at the base of the neck.

4.   Swiftly run your fingers down along the spine (from the base of the neck to the sacrum) about twenty times.

5.   Find the indentations on the sacrum and again use the thumb and index finger of one hand to draw parallel power symbols there. This helps the Reiki flow through both the upper and lower body of the client.

6.   Divide the upper part of the back into six areas,

three on each side of the spine. Place your palms on the upper area on either side of the spine and brush your hands out to the sides of the body, and then do the same to the remaining parts. Repeat this three to four times.

7. Brush across the small of the back, rubbing your hand from side to side with slight pressure about ten times.

8. Start at the hip and sweep your hand down along the outside of the leg to the ankle. Repeat three to four times, and then do the same on the other leg.

9. Start from the back of the thigh and sweep your hand down the back of the leg to the ankle. Repeat three to four times, and then do the same on the other leg.

10. Start from the inside of the lower thigh and sweep your hand down to the ankle. Repeat three to four times, and then do the same on the other leg.

11. Pushing down on the base of the thigh just above the back of the knee with one hand, clasp the ankle with your other hand. Using your body weight, gently stretch the back of the knee. Repeat the same procedure with the other leg.

12. Pat the back all over from the upper to the lower torso. Repeat three to four times.

13. Pat down the legs in the same order as steps 8-10. Begin with the outside of the leg, then do the back of the leg, and then the inside of the leg (alternating right and left legs).

Exploring and Working with Bodily Pain

Reiki can be effective in working with bodily pain in the following ways:

1. Exploring physical pain;

2. Bringing insight and awareness into the cause of pain;

3. Releasing pain;

4. Speeding up the body's healing process after injury or surgery; and

5. Helping to manage symptoms of stress that often accompany chronic pain (e.g., sleep disturbance, fatigue, headaches, poor concentration, shortness of breath, increased muscle tension, anxiety, and depression).

Applying Reiki directly to areas of pain has the capability of reducing and relieving the pain itself. Levine (1987) states that touch itself can ease pain: the Gate Theory of pain teaches that "soft touch in an area of hard injury can confuse the pain's signals through the 'neural gate,' a phenomenon by which lesser sensations are able to displace the more intense by gently occupying the same message pathway to the pain receptors in the brain" (Levine, 1987, p. 65).

To begin the process of helping a client to manage her pain, have the client turn her attention toward the pain with awareness and acceptance, allowing it to be as it is. As the client enters into the sensations of the pain, try to have her identify the way the body tenses and constricts around the pain, and notice the mental and emotional reactions she is having to the pain. These reactions often serve to intensify and exacerbate physical pain.

With intentional focus, you can direct the client to bring to mind the specific thoughts and emotions that are contributing to her experience of physical pain, and begin to work on letting these go. You can help the client to construct corrective and soothing thoughts and affirmations for healing and for pain relief. Then you can use Reiki to install these messages in the area of the client's pain, using the Reiki power symbol to seal in the messages.

I have also found it effective to have clients visualize healing the area of injury while I am giving them Reiki. Give Reiki to the area of the client's pain and instruct her to breathe into and out of this area. Have her focus her attention on the flow of the Reiki and visualize the Reiki energy softening, easing and dissolving the pain. As much as she can, have the client focus her awareness on the breath and notice any thoughts, emotions, or sensations that arise. This approach encourages the client to relate to her pain rather than react from it, and to approach the pain in a calmer, more relaxed way.

The Relaxation Response

Dr. Margaret Caudill (2009), a pain management specialist and co-director at Beth Israel Deaconess Medical Center in Boston, Massachusetts, has written a book called *Managing Pain Before it Manages You*. In it, she cites significant research support for using the relaxation response to help people manage pain and the fear that pain stimulates.

When the relaxation response is activated, the heart rate and blood pressure drop and the need for oxygen decreases, which slows down the breath. In her book *Minding the Body, Mending the Mind*, Joan Borysenko (1987) writes, "Brain waves shift from an alert beta rhythm to a relaxed alpha or theta rhythm. Blood flow to the muscles decreases, and instead, blood is sent to the brain and skin, producing a feeling of warmth and rested mental alertness" (Borysenko, 1987, p. 17).

In treatment for pain management, the relaxation response can be activated by the practitioner giving Reiki to the back of the client's head. Instruct the client to take a detached approach to the thoughts, feelings and sensations that arise around his pain. Remind him not to engage with them, just allow them to come and go. In Caudill's (2009) experience, the things we tell ourselves about the pain we are experiencing often serve to intensify the pain (e.g., "I'll never get over this," "It will never stop," or "I can't stand this."). Therefore, you can work to help your client monitor his thoughts using Reiki, and can install corrective messages if that is helpful.

It is also useful to teach clients Reiki so they can induce the relaxation response on their own for twenty minutes per day for pain management, stress reduction, anxiety management, and developing presence within the body.

Directed Attention

One method for exploring and releasing pain is the use of directed attention. While giving Reiki, have the client focus his attention on the inner energy field of the body and connect to the aliveness of this energy flow. Then instruct the client to ask the body-mind to reveal the source of the pain he feels and the places that most need healing in order to resolve it. The site of the pain is not necessarily the location of the underlying imbalance causing the pain. This exercise frequently brings out memories of unresolved pain that the client was previously unaware of, but which need healing.

Bodily sensations, including physical pain, may be expressing unreleased emotion or mental or relational conflict. While giving your client Reiki, have him enter into an area of bodily pain and use his attention to identify and describe the qualities of the pain: its shape, size, color, texture and any thoughts, emotions or memories it is holding or symbolizing.

As I mentioned in this book's introduction, in my first experiences with receiving Reiki treatments, when I directed my attention into an area of abdominal pain I discovered that this pain was actually the sensation of unreleased traumatic memories from childhood. As I opened to and allowed my feelings, sensations, emotions and thoughts to arise and express themselves in the abdomen, I began to retrieve forgotten memories of violent childhood scenes. After accessing and allowing these memories to surface, the physical pain went away.

CASE EXAMPLE

I used the directed attention exercise with a client I was giving Reiki to when he began to feel pain in his knee. This turned out to be an area he'd had surgery on many years ago, and although the knee was now physically healed, it was still holding trauma energy from the surgery. Giving Reiki to the knee brought back emotional memories of the surgery and released the trauma energy that was stored there, alleviating my client's pain.

Personal Assessment Process

A method for exploring and releasing pain or discomfort is discussed by Earlene Gleisner (1992) in her book *Reiki in Everyday Living*. She outlines four steps, Recognize, Reveal, Explore and Release, which can be combined with Reiki for effective healing in the following ways:

1. *Recognize*: While giving your client Reiki, help him become aware of the part of the body that is in tension or in pain (e.g., sore throat, headache, abdominal pain, etc.).

2. *Reveal*: Have him identify and name the emotion that is expressing itself as tension or pain in this part of the body.

3. *Explore*: Pain in a specific body part can be reinforced by one or more memories. While giving Reiki to that body part, have the client ask that a picture of the original trauma reveal itself, and have him consider what recently happened to trigger this pain.

4. *Release*: Help the client have gratitude for the insight and clarity, and release the hold this past experience has on his present life. Have the client send loving kindness to the injury, to himself and to his body.

CASE EXAMPLE

Giving Reiki to the head of a woman with migraine headaches revealed that her head "ached with worries." Exploring these worries, we found their origins came from a childhood where she had grown up in an environment of chronic tension. Reiki treatments helped to clear the energetic charge underlying these memories.

The egoic mind is the conditioned mind with all of its ideas, attitudes, thoughts and beliefs floating in the sky of consciousness.

CHAPTER 5

Working with the Mind

A basic practice in working with the mind is teaching clients to observe and assess the nature and quality of their thoughts and to understand how these thoughts are contributing to their symptoms. When we talk about working with the mind, we are really talking about that aspect of the mind called ego. The ego is the conditioned mind with all of its ideas, attitudes, thoughts and beliefs about who we are (our personality), who others are, how we relate to others, and how the world operates.

The egoic mind is also the thinking mind, and most of our thoughts are a product of our conditioning, what we have been taught and what we have experienced, and the meaning we make of these experiences. It is observable that although we are able to direct our thoughts, our thoughts often direct us. It is as if thinking "thinks" us. It is an automatic process. Thinking just seems to happen in a steady stream, thought after thought, and it is almost impossible to stop this stream and to not think. The expression "the mind has a mind of its own" refers to the habitual way the mind has been conditioned to think its thoughts without our direction.

Furthermore, it is clinically observable that the egoic mind tends to cling to its conditioning and has difficulty changing its mind even in the face of changing conditions. For example, if as a child a traumatic experience makes you conclude that the world is a dangerous place, it is likely that this belief will persist into adulthood even when your life's circumstances are relatively safe. The egoic mind tends to find data to support and perpetuate its original thoughts and beliefs and to ignore current data that contradicts it, so that even when our present life is better, the conditioning from the past persists. The mind churns out what it has come to believe, regardless of the validity or the reliability of these beliefs.

Consciousness

Fortunately, the egoic mind is not the only dimension of mind that there is. There is also an alert and intelligent presence within us that is consciousness itself (Tolle, 1999, 2005). Thoughts arise within the space of consciousness, but consciousness does not create thought; our conditioning does. Consciousness is pure awareness without thought, and when we align ourselves with this state we can detach from the egoic mind and observe its functioning without identifying with it. One particular practice that utilizes this conscious presence to work with the egoic mind is mindfulness.

Reiki and Mindfulness

Mindfulness is the practice of being present with one's ongoing experience in a non-judgmental and self-accepting way (Germer, Siegel & Fulton, 2005). It is the willingness to allow whatever images, thoughts, emotions or bodily sensations that arise to be just as they are. The value of using this practice in working with the mind's conditioning is that we cannot begin to modify the mind if we don't first see what it is up to.

Normally when we have an idea, a thought, an image or an emotion we immediately identify it as "me" or "mine." We align with it. We enter into relationship with it. There is a kind of ownership that happens whether the experience is positive, neutral or negative. As this identification process repeats itself over and over, in time we build an identity around our relationship with our thoughts. These thoughts and ideas become who we think we are and who we think we are not.

Central to the practice of mindfulness is learning to allow the arising of thoughts, ideas and emotions without identifying them as "me" or "mine" or even "not me" and "not mine." Allowing means having no relationship, no ownership of these thoughts or emotions as they come and go. We don't take them personally. Instead, we experience these thoughts as mind movements determined by our conditioning.

Mindfulness gives us the perspective that we are that which is aware of our thoughts, that we are awareness itself. When clients learn to observe and detach from their symptomatic thoughts they are in a better position to see where these thoughts originated, and to assess the nature and quality of them and their validity and truthfulness. By identifying self-defeating, self-limiting, erroneous or conditioned thoughts, we can edit, correct or modify them and install corrective, healthy replacements.

Reiki treatments support the practice of mindfulness in several ways. First, Reiki helps to focus attention, increase awareness and promote insight into the nature of the egoic mind's predominant thoughts and thought patterns. Second, Reiki helps to quiet the mind by bringing the mind into conscious, sensory contact with presence and the field of Ki. Quieting the mind makes the mind more receptive to change. Third, when we hold our symptoms in the light of consciousness while receiving Reiki, we alter our relationship to them. It ceases to be "my thought" and becomes thought, it ceases to be "my anxiety" and becomes the non-personal experience of anxiety, anxiety everyone feels. Allowing our symptoms to be in the energy of Reiki and with non-attachment allows them to release their hold on us and to transform.

While giving Reiki to the back of your client's head, have your client ask herself how her mind is perceiving her current predicament, problem or symptom. Have her discuss with you her mind's view of the problem. This exercise can help your client to see that her mind's perspective on a certain problem is not the only perspective.

CASE EXAMPLES

David was very depressed and felt anxious and sad, but was unable to see any cause or understand why because his life was going pretty well. He began to mindfully track his thoughts during Reiki treatments and was able to identify the self-defeating thinking that made him approach life with the constant expectation of trouble. Therapy helped him work with the conditioning that led to this thinking and helped him to modify it.

For many people, watching the mind and learning to dis-identify with being the mind is in itself very healing. Jean thought of herself as "bad," as a bad person. Reiki helped her to mindfully observe these thoughts and to dis-identify with them. She began to see how she had been conditioned to believe that she was bad and to understand that this conclusion was just the result of conditioning and not the truth. Over the course of several months, she developed greater compassion for herself and a better self-image, and was able to alter her mind's negative beliefs.

Gassho Meditation

In his Reiki classes, Usui taught his students a form of mindfulness meditation called Gassho meditation. Presumably, he was training his students to experience the "witness state" of conscious presence in which thoughts, emotions and sensations arise and fall away. Usui had his students practice Gassho meditation at the beginning of his Reiki workshops, and he recommended that his students practice Gassho for twenty to thirty minutes after getting up in the morning and before going to bed in the evening (Usui & Petter, 1999).

Once a practitioner has been attuned to Reiki, practicing Gassho meditation has several benefits. It sensitizes the practitioner's hands to feeling the sensations and flow of Reiki passing through them, and it increases the practitioner's skill at applying Reiki as an open channel without the mind's involvement and without allowing her thoughts, feelings or sensations to intrude.

To practice Gassho meditation, set yourself in a sitting position that allows you to be alert and relaxed. Close your eyes and place your hands together in a prayer position in front of your heart. Focus your entire attention at the point where your two middle fingers meet. Try to forget everything else. If a thought or an emotion arises, note it, let it go and refocus your attention on the sensation between your middle fingers.

Finding the Source of a Problem

At times, clients will need help clarifying the nature of a problem, and understanding its root cause and how it developed over time. A useful exercise for finding the source of a problem is discussed by Thondup (1996).

While giving the client a Reiki treatment, instruct him to relax his body and mind. Tell him to take a few deep breaths and imagine that all his worries are being released on the exhale. Ask him to feel peaceful and calm and to relax in this space for a while. Then, when he is ready, have him bring the problem to mind. Have him see it, feel it and acknowledge its presence, and remember when, where and how this problem began. Guide him back to the earliest possible time, place and source of the problem.

By contemplating the causes and feelings of a problem, we are already helping to heal it. Going back through the past broadens our perspective and because of the effects of time, we feel less anxiety about the problem in the present. By going to the root, we catch the problem at its source. We work with the cause as it reveals itself in the present, and we develop compassion toward ourselves and others in the process. For example, if our parents harmed us, we see this clearly and at the same time we see the injuries they themselves were raised with, and our perspective broadens.

We should work to see our problems objectively and not judge or label them negatively, and Reiki can help us do this. In healing, no emotion is wrong or needs to be denied. We accept the existence of our feelings, welcome them and allow them to surface so that they can then be released (Thondup, 1996).

Working with Problematic Thoughts and Beliefs

A thought believed has great power. Thoughts don't

have to be true; we just have to *believe* they are true. Once a thought is believed, it is powered by our conviction and intention. Our thoughts and beliefs form the filter through which we strain reality. We don't see reality; we see what we believe reality to be and then organize ourselves around this. Our actions are based upon these core thoughts and beliefs.

Many of our psychological and emotional symptoms are rooted in problematic thoughts and beliefs: fear-producing thoughts, critical judgments, self-defeating thoughts, self-limiting beliefs, erroneously constructed cause-effect relationships, and depressed thoughts, to name just a few. A belief may also reflect "old-world" thinking (i.e., it was true at one time, in the past, but is no longer true).

Thoughts and beliefs are energies, and when we personalize them we make them "mine." When we depersonalize them by detaching and witnessing them as forms of energy, we are in a position to examine them as conditioned responses and to evaluate their accuracy or truthfulness. We can begin exploring the root causes of problematic judgments and faulty cognitive constructs.

We can speak directly with our problematic thoughts and beliefs through therapeutic dialoguing techniques. Byron Katie (2007) is a contemporary spiritual teacher who helps people work with their psychological pain by learning to question the thoughts that create it. She developed a method of inquiry she calls "The Work."

The Work consists of using four questions to investigate problematic beliefs:

1. *Is it true?*

2. *Can you absolutely know that it's true?*

3. *How do you react when you believe that thought?*

4. *Who would you be without that thought?* (Katie, 2007, p. xiii)

One approach you can use during a Reiki treatment session, while following the standard hand positions, is to instruct your client to invite in or focus on a negative thought or belief. Have him contemplate each of the four questions in sequence, taking as much time as needed with each one. Talk these questions out with him. Have your client pay attention to where this belief is living in his body and to the emotions and bodily sensations this thought or belief generates. Have him notice how a belief stirs emotion and how this emotion generates more thoughts.

Additional questions for his self-exploration might include:

- *What is it like to live with this belief?*
- *What stops me from letting go of this belief?*
- *What is the origin of this belief?*
- *What function does this belief serve?*
- *How does it help?*
- *How does it hinder?*

Another method for examining and working with problematic thoughts is called RAIN.

RAIN: A Mindfulness Tool

Tara Brach (2012) describes a four-step process using the acronym RAIN to decondition a habitual response to a symptom or symptom cluster. Like the NAOR method described earlier in this book, RAIN teaches us to stop and attend to an emerging symptom with mindful attention and presence.

The four steps of RAIN are:

Recognize what is happening.

Allow life to be just as it is.

Investigate inner experience with kindness.

Non-Identification (i.e., your identity is not fused with or defined by your habitual response) (Brach, 2012, p. 62).

These four steps are a valuable template for guiding a client through a mindful investigation of how she responds to a stressful event, a recurring emotional problem or a negative thought pattern. In preparation for this exercise, be sure to put the mental-emotional Reiki symbol, covered by the power symbol, in your hands. The mental-emotional symbol is particularly helpful in altering conditioned patterns.

CASE EXAMPLE

Donna suffered from frequent bouts of anxiety that lasted several hours to several days. In the course of psychotherapy she had uncovered issues that triggered her anxiety but this insight alone was not preventing it. The focus of this particular session was to explore the anxiety itself, how it was operating in her and how to manage it better.

As I applied Reiki to the back of Donna's head, I encouraged her to connect with the feeling and the flow of Reiki. Once she was feeling the Reiki's effect, I had her bring to mind a recent work situation that aroused her anxiety. As she focused on this situation she began to feel anxious, and as the anxiety grew stronger she noticed she was becoming afraid of it.

I encouraged Donna to shift her attention from the experience of anxiety to the fear-producing thoughts she was having about the anxiety: "I hate this feeling, it's just going to get stronger," "Once it starts it won't stop," "It's going to wreck my whole day," and "I must be crazy." I directed Donna to witness these thoughts without trying to engage with them, to just try to be present with the thoughts and with the anxiety. I had her describe the sensations they were generating within her body.

When the anxiety became too strong I had Donna shift her focus to following her breath and to holding herself in kindness and compassion. As I continued to apply Reiki, following the standard hand positions, I encouraged Donna to shift her perspective from *being* her anxiety and her fearful thoughts to *having* them. I helped her to recognize that the anxiety and the thoughts she was experiencing were the result of her conditioning and not because she was inadequate, "bad" or "crazy." Understanding that we are not the symptoms we are experiencing is a first step in bringing about their transformation. During our session, I encouraged Donna to recognize that the anxiety she feels and the mind's reactions to it are part of being human, part of our common humanity. It often helps to calm the body when we can see the universal in our symptoms.

As the session progressed Donna noticed that her anxiety was subsiding and she felt more grounded in her body. She noted two positive outcomes from the session. First, holding her symptoms in kindness and with compassion was helpful in calming them. Second, she had the insight that regardless of what triggered her anxiety, once the anxiety was present her mind started producing fearful thoughts about it, and these thoughts "grew" and fed the anxiety. The four steps of RAIN helped Donna to alter her perspective from being "caught" in her anxiety to witnessing the anxiety and relating to it with mindful self-compassion.

RAIN and Obsessive Thinking

Brach (2012) also suggests using RAIN to investigate the problem of obsessive thinking. First, have your client identify a theme that his mind routinely obsesses about (for example, how people are treating him, mistakes he is making, what he needs to get done, what others are doing wrong, how he looks, what is going to go wrong, what has already gone wrong, how he needs to change, how others need to change). Second, while giving your client Reiki, have him focus on this issue and guide him through each of the four steps of RAIN.

The energy of Reiki creates a space between ourselves and our thoughts, which enables us to detach from our thoughts and to see them from a witness perspective. Holding our thoughts in the compassionate energy of Reiki allows awareness to loosen the grip of the mind's compulsive beliefs and judgments, and over time to assist in their transformation.

Quieting the Mind

At times it is helpful to distract the mind and to withdraw attention from thought by focusing our attention elsewhere. Focusing attention on the body quiets the mind. Have your client try directing his attention to following the breath, attending to the sensation of the energy field of his inner body, feeling the flow of Reiki, or noticing what his senses are perceiving in the present.

One way to do this is to have him mindfully connect with each part of his body as you give Reiki to his head.

While tuning into the Reiki energy, he can use the body scan technique to focus his attention on each area, beginning at the top of his head and moving slowly down his neck, shoulders and torso to his arms, hands, legs and feet, following the flow of Reiki. The repetition of mantras, and meditations like the metta meditation, are also useful in pulling the mind away from whatever it is dwelling upon. Quieting the mind opens us to the experience of the heart, and a deeper connection to our true selves.

Bringing Presence to a Fearful Thought or Memory

Have your client bring to mind a fearful thought, image or memory while you give her Reiki. Instruct her to hold this thought, focus on it and allow it to develop as best she can while remaining grounded. Now have her shift her attention to the field of awareness in which this thought exists. Have her open her attention to all of her senses and rest in the awareness of being.

Have her notice the difference between *being* and *thinking*. Allowing the thought to be just as it is, without reacting to it, expresses the "being" mode, whereas thinking is an ego function and puts us in the "doing" mode. When we think a fear-producing thought, we will experience the impulse or desire to do something about it even when there is nothing to be done. The physiological effect of thinking we have to do something when nothing can be done induces a stress response in the body; it is like stepping on the gas and the brake at the same time while driving a car. When we rest in the awareness of the thought without taking action, we take our foot off the accelerator.

Tolle (2005) discusses the deep feeling of peace that can be accessed in the energy field of the present moment. As your client holds the fearful thought in presence, have her allow the peace of the present moment to settle into the fearful thought. She will notice that the fearful thought, image or memory will begin to lose its power and diminish in intensity. When we hold our fear in the state of presence, we access the energy field's healing potential and often release the symptom.

Working with a Negative Storyline or Mental Construction

Shainberg (2000) tells the story in *Chasing Elephants* of a client who has a longing for a partner but can never sustain a relationship long enough to keep one. The client has a story she tells herself about what a "loser" she is, how unworthy she is, how she'll be alone and lonely all her life. This story terrifies her and keeps her in anxiety and despair, and she is constantly walking around thinking about her situation and feeling anger and self-hatred.

Shainberg (2000) states that the healing for this mental construction or storyline is to have this client feel the anger when it arises in her body, stay present with the pain and the hurt underneath the anger, give them a space to exist, and send compassion into her pain. As this client stays present with her pain, opens to it and lets go of the mental concepts around it, it is likely that she will understand the original causes and conditions of her present-day problem, and will be able to recognize the "well" of emotion that her present-day problem is triggering.

This method of working with a negative storyline is easily adapted to Reiki treatment. To do this, have the client bring up and focus on the story he is telling himself and talk it out with you while you give him Reiki. The Reiki energy helps to ground the client and anchor his awareness in the body. Once the problem is laid out, have the client focus on his feelings and the movement of energy inside his body, have him pay attention to his experience, and have him send compassion and loving kindness to himself.

The Reiki energy brings clarity and insight to the problem and can help the client understand how and why the story developed. Grounding this mental-emotional process in the body often results in the client's ability to let go of the story.

Releasing the Energetic Charge Underlying Trauma and Stress

Stress reactions are characterized by the body-mind going into fight, flight or freeze mode in response to a threat or the perception of a threat. What one considers threatening is dependent upon one's conditioning and life experience. Threat may be perceived in practically anything. (See Chapter 9 for additional information about stress reactions.)

Traumatic experience and stress reactions leave people

with a multiplex of symptoms that affect cognition, emotion and behavior. Examples include intrusive thoughts and memories, intense and painful emotions, avoidance and resistance, and fight, flight or freeze behavior. When these reactions are not cleared or released at the time of the trauma, the flow of Ki energy will vitalize these symptoms and store them like a "program" in the body and in the H.E.F. This program is reactivated whenever the person experiences an event or situation that triggers her to the original trauma or stress.

Reiki is helpful in releasing this program and installing a corrective one. The process of clearing and re-setting the H.E.F. to a new program is similar to the procedure you follow for setting your car radio to a particular station. Once you tune into the station you want, you push in the station selection button and hold it until you hear the beep, and then the new station is programmed into the radio.

To reset the H.E.F., have the client bring to mind the problem "program" and hold this while you give her Reiki using the standard hand positions, starting at the head (these positions connect to certain key energy points that are involved in the storage of mental and emotional information). As you move through the series of hand positions, the client will generally experience the problem program fading. Clients often experience this as losing interest in thinking about the problem, or as feeling the intense emotion subsiding.

Once the client has released as much as she is going to

in this session, you can then install corrective information using the Sei He Ki technique. Corrective programming can include the use of healing affirmations, pleasant feelings and scenes, positive and functional thoughts, etc. You can install corrective information in particular chakras that are related to the problem program or to the heart and the solar plexus chakras. I have also had clients use the phrase format from The Emotional Freedom Technique as an installation: "Even though I have this _____, I deeply love and accept myself" (Feinstein, Eden & Craig, 2005, p. 38).

Creating and Using Affirmations

Creating and using affirmations and healing meditations help to direct the Reiki energy and focus both practitioners and clients on specific outcomes. They may be geared toward the client's well-being in general or may be specific to a client's particular problem.

For example, I often silently repeat a version of the Buddhist loving kindness meditation during a Reiki treatment:

May you dwell in your heart.
May you be free from suffering.
May you be healed.
May you be at peace. (Levine, 1987, p. 25)

Or, when working with a client in recovery from trauma, I often use this statement: "May the effects that remain from the trauma you have endured be released from the cells of your body and your energy field now."

To focus on a specific target or outcome, a client and I will create an affirmation to use together throughout a Reiki treatment session.

Some examples include:

•   "Getting in touch with my soul, I release old habits and create healthy new ones."

•   "My body is healthy, ready to conceive and able to support a full-term pregnancy."

•   "May the Reiki energy sweep through the cells of my body and bring healing to any imbalance within me."

•   "I am free from worry and embrace the day."

Some Keys in Creating Affirmations

When creating affirmations to work with, here are some helpful guidelines to follow, as outlined by Serge King (1981) in his *Imagineering for Health: Self-Healing through the Use of the Mind*:

1.   Keep affirmations short and direct.

2.   Make them specific enough to have a clear meaning for you.

3.   Affirmations are most effective when they focus on changing beliefs you have about yourself or about life in general (i.e., instead of telling yourself, "I always get sick this time of year," state "I'm always healthy").

4.   Word affirmations in positive terms (i.e., use "I'm always healthy" instead of "I never get sick"). If you use negative words, then negative images often arise in your

mind and can influence your subconscious.

5. An effective affirmation is one that has at least some believability and credibility. If you create an affirmation that is unrealistic or counters your beliefs, the chances of it working are slim. For example, if you are seriously ill, saying, "I'm perfectly healthy" is counterproductive and pointless. If you choose to say, "I *can* be perfectly healthy," that has a much better chance of taking effect.

6. The most effective phrase to place in an affirmation is "I can." It opens up the possibility that what you want to be or do is within reach, and as the affirmation becomes habitual, your thought patterns will change and it will work.

In summary, good affirmations are short, clear, specific, positive and believable.

Installing Affirmations: The Sei He Ki Technique

The fourth therapeutic task, Installing Corrective Experience, often focuses on the mind and the mind's mental constructions. The client and practitioner co-create corrective beliefs, thoughts, attitudes, scenes, and affirmations to install during a Reiki treatment.

Usui taught particular hand positions to be used when installing information in a client's field, called the Sei He Ki technique. The Sei He Ki technique requires the use of the three Reiki Level Two symbols. After placing these symbols in his hands, the therapist places his dominant hand on the back of the client's head and his non-dominant hand on the client's forehead. The therapist keeps his hands there for two or three minutes while both he and the client silently repeat the affirmation. Then, the therapist removes his non-dominant hand from the client's forehead and continues to give Reiki to the back of the client's head (Lübeck, Petter & Rand, 2001).

I have also found it effective when both the client and therapist repeat an agreed upon affirmation or healing meditation throughout the course of a whole body treatment.

CASE EXAMPLE

Vicky was with a group of women friends over the weekend when she got triggered by memories and feelings of being rejected and teased by peers in junior high school. She felt so uncomfortable that she got up and left. When she came in for her next session, we used Reiki to explore these memories, to connect them to feelings from her past and to release the charge underlying these memories and feelings. We then used the Sei He Ki technique to install corrective thoughts such as, "I'm likeable," "I'm deserving of love and attention," and "I'm good enough." This exercise helped Vicky to resolve unfinished business from the past and find greater ease in social situations.

Emotional work is directed at either releasing the charge underlying a toxic emotion or draining the "well" of stored emotional pain.

CHAPTER 6

Working with Emotion

From the perspective of Psychotherapeutic Reiki, there are two related points that are important to keep in mind while working with emotional problems. The first point is that emotion is understood to be "the body's reaction to the mind" (Tolle, 2005, p. 132). Thoughts generate chemical reactions in the body that are experienced as physiological events which we learn to label as particular emotions. For example, during a nightmare your body reacts as if you are experiencing the nightmare's events. Or when you find yourself thinking about an upcoming stressful event, your body tenses, becomes anxious or goes into flight-or-fight mode even though the upcoming event has not yet happened. The second point is that chronic and unreleased emotions are stored throughout the body and must be treated in the body in order to be released (Pert, 2004, 2011).

Because of these two points, most emotional work is directed at either modifying and restructuring cognitive processes, or releasing the emotional effects of stress, negative conditioning, unresolved trauma or physical illness and pain by treating the body where the emotion resides.

When working with emotional issues, you can help the client discover the original source of their emotional pain and the relationship between particular thoughts and particular emotions, while also paying attention to where in the body these emotions are located. One way to do this is to help the client track the thoughts that occur before and during an emotional reaction in order to help assess the cause and effect relationship between thought and emotion.

Unreleased and Unresolved Emotion

Expressing emotion is different from releasing emotion. Whereas expressing emotion is the act of discharging a feeling in response to a current trigger, releasing emotion involves conscious connection with the source of the trigger: the original trauma. This original trauma carries with it a "well" of emotional pain that current-day triggers continually tap into. For example, when we express anger without awareness of its deeper source, we are simply venting the anger. Although that emotion will temporarily run its course, it will be triggered again by any situation that consciously or unconsciously reminds us of the original trauma. Venting alone gets us no closer to understanding, resolving or releasing the effects of the original trauma. In order to fully release emotional pain, we need to discover its source.

Unresolved emotion that is carried and stored in the

body and energy field is mostly an accumulation of the bits and pieces of unexamined and unexpressed emotional pain from the many traumas, abuses and losses we endured while growing up. Some of these traumas are big but many of them are small: assaults to our self-esteem, the devaluing or ignoring of certain basic needs, boundary and dignity violations, ridicule, being spanked or hit, punishments that exceeded our capacity to handle them, unfairness, discrimination, or painful losses such as having to move away from a beloved home, secure neighborhood and close friends.

My wife, Amanda Curtin, is a clinical social worker specializing in treatment groups for adults who grew up in difficult circumstances and dysfunctional families. She refers to the above-mentioned types of traumas as "everyday trauma." In an unpublished article titled, "The Everyday Trauma Recovery Model," she defines everyday trauma as the accumulation of emotional wounds initially experienced in childhood but then added to over the course of the life cycle.

There are people who attend Amanda's groups who grew up in clean, middle class houses, had functioning and involved parents, had enough money to have their needs provided for – all the material stuff of happiness. Yet when they take the time to deeply examine their childhood experiences, they remember times when they were scared, angry, hurt or sad and unable to express these feelings, which became bottled up inside.

For example, one girl had a mother who was emotionally distant, a mother whom she experienced as uncaring. Because children tend to take things personally and blame themselves for how they are treated, this girl grew up to believe that she wasn't cared about because she was (and still is) unlovable. Another example is illustrated by a man who as a boy was continually trying to please his father but never got the approval he was seeking, no matter his accomplishments. As an adult, this man describes himself as a perfectionist, a workaholic who continually strives to accomplish at the expense of having distant relationships with his wife and children.

These case examples are typical of the normal kinds of experiences most of us have growing up. Unfortunately, and all too often, we are discouraged from discussing and expressing our emotional reactions. We are conditioned to either minimize or suppress them, or take them in stride, get over them and move on.

In his book *Unattended Sorrow,* Levine (2005) discusses the psychological and emotional costs that accrue when we turn away from emotional pain and sorrow or don't adequately grieve a loss. He makes the point that when we don't attend to our emotions, when we close off from them, we are closing off from parts of ourselves. Essentially, these emotional reactions, no matter how small, become buried, intensify, and in time begin to manifest in unexpected ways. They can "weaken the body . . . compartmentalize the mind . . . disturb our sleep . . . sap our energy . . . inhibit our intuition . . . numb sexuality or turn it frantic," decrease our ability to trust, slow our creativity, and foster addictions (Levine, 2005, p. 4). Unexpressed emotions can also cause us to hide in relationships rather than face the pain, and can narrow the path of our lives by creating a distrust of the future and a loss of confidence in what lies ahead (Levine, 2005).

As time goes by and development unfolds, the emotional effects of unexamined and unexpressed emotional pain become woven into the fabric of our personality. As mentioned, these effects are stored and carried in the body and energy field and eventually can express through symptoms we don't understand and are unable to correlate with our current life experience.

One of the greatest benefits of Reiki is that it helps to surface and clear the emotional holdings we carry within. It is a common occurrence that during a Reiki treatment people experience a fleeting image or memory from some emotionally painful event from the past. Like a shooting star that suddenly appears and passes through the night sky, these memories surface and quickly fade.

In this instance, the Reiki is finding the energy block created by an emotionally charged memory and removing the charge underlying that memory, thereby allowing it to be released. As this happens, many people experience a feeling of peace. Over the course of multiple treatments the accumulated "well" of emotionally charged memories begins to diminish and not only do clients begin to feel a greater sense of well-being, but the abilities and capabilities that were suppressed begin to re-emerge.

Cell Memory

A related perspective for understanding the effect of unresolved emotion is cell memory. When a traumatic event is not fully processed or resolved and the emotional reactions are not fully discharged, the unintegrated aspects of the trauma remain in the body and the H.E.F. These unresolved reactions are imprinted and stored in the cells of the body. As each generation of cells die out and are replaced by new ones, the traumatic emotional reactions imprinted in them are passed on to the next generation. If untreated, these emotions can lead to chronic disorders and to stress reactions that impair the health of the physical body.

According to Candice Pert (2011), "No matter how much conscious work you do to change your cellular patterns, your emotions are stored in your body and it is in your body that they must be addressed. Seek out a bodyworker to help you revitalize the physical processes that will restore you to wholeness" (p. 11).

Reiki treatments are helpful in releasing energy blockages, and in balancing and vitalizing the physical body and H.E.F. Applying Reiki while the client is experiencing a negative emotion can decrease the intensity of that emotion and bring out sensations in the parts of the body that store and carry the emotion. "Negative emotion" refers to emotion that is toxic to the body and disrupts the flow of Ki in the energy field. Chronic worry, anxiety, anger, sadness, shame or depression can all be considered negative emotions in this sense.

Case Example

Diane wanted to start a home Internet business but whenever she sat down to work on this, she became fearful, anxious and blocked in her efforts. While giving her Reiki, I asked her to let herself feel the fearfulness she had about starting this business. As her feelings of fear arose she located them in her solar plexus. I moved to her solar plexus and as I gave her Reiki, I asked her to allow the solar plexus to reveal the underlying nature of her fear.

Diane had the idea of not being deserving of having success, and she could immediately connect this idea to many childhood incidents and to her childhood conditioning. Over the course of several sessions we focused on these incidents and the feelings they brought up in order to help release them. We then installed the corrective affirmation, "I am deserving of having my own business and of being successful." After our work together, Diane was then able to move forward with her business idea.

A Mindful Approach to Working with Emotion

Kornfield (2011) writes that a mindful way of working with any emotion is not to push it away but to turn our attention toward it, experience it in the body and mind, stay with it and gently name it. In this way, we learn to be fully aware of that emotional state without being so caught up in it. Then we can choose which way to go and which impulses to follow in working with it.

For example, you may have to acknowledge fear numerous times before the emotion becomes fully identifiable. If you are willing to sit quietly and acknowledge when the fear arises, greeting it rather than fighting or repressing it, you begin to recognize it as a passing emotion. This enables a detachment that helps us to develop a wiser relationship with the emotion, rather than becoming overwhelmed by it (Kornfield, 2011).

Kornfield (2011) writes, "Anger, fear, desire – all these states can be a source of wisdom when they are acknowledged and felt fully. As we become more present for them, we see how they arise according to certain conditions and affect the body and mind in certain ways" (p. 78). If we can train ourselves to become mindful of these emotions rather than getting caught up in them, we can learn to observe them and subsequently learn from them.

CASE EXAMPLE

Doug suffered from generalized anxiety disorder and was prone to feeling unexpected upsurges of anxiety that would last from seconds to minutes before they would pass away. These spikes of anxiety could be triggered by a sudden, unbidden and intrusive thought or memory, sensory stimuli (a certain sound or smell), or interactions with other people. He felt "ambushed" by these surges. They were distracting and disturbing because they took his attention away from whatever he had been doing, and he was afraid of them. He feared that they would get worse or cause him to have a heart attack, although so far they had not.

In therapy, Doug and I worked on understanding that these anxiety "attacks" were transitory phenomena expressing the unreleased effects of past conditioning and triggered by current associated stimuli. We processed that he actually was not getting worse; rather, he was discharging the emotional energy he carried in the body and energy field. I taught him that fighting with and resisting these upsurges only served to strengthen them, or at least allowed them to continue.

In time, when one of these spikes occurred, he practiced naming it "anxiety" and just letting it pass through him like a wave without resisting it. Although he could not always stop his catastrophic thoughts, he practiced not taking them seriously, nor identifying them as true. The image of an ocean wave helped him experience the feeling, allow it, and let it pass through without getting the mind involved.

Emotional Flooding

Prior to working with emotion, especially when you are using exposure techniques that may elicit strong emotional reactions in your client, you need to assess your client's ability to manage emotional intensity. If necessary, help your client develop the emotional regulation skills that will enable him to maintain a feeling of control when exposed to strong emotion. Strong emotion tends to be energetically unbalancing and can create sensations of feeling pulled out of one's body (e.g., light-headedness, disorientation or disassociation). The more grounded your client is in his body, the better able he will be to tolerate, relate to and work with emotion when it arises.

The energy of Reiki is an effective anchor for grounding and this is a primary reason for acclimating your client to Reiki prior to bringing up symptoms. Other anchors that are helpful for grounding include abdominal breathing, directed attention, visualization, mindfulness, and heartfulness practices, which are discussed in other chapters.

Still, there may be occasion when your client's emotional experience is intense, and he fears it might be overwhelming. If your client is feeling emotionally flooded, place one hand on his heart chakra and the other just above his navel center, on his solar plexus chakra. Direct him to begin abdominal breathing and to focus his attention on the physical sensations he is feeling in his body beneath your hands. Have him attend to the rise and fall of the breath in his solar plexus and abdomen. It may be helpful to direct him to silently repeat a calming phrase or meditation, such as Thich Nhat Hanh's "Breathing in, I calm the activities of body and mind. . . Breathing out, I smile" (Hanh, 1991, p. 23).

Instruct your client to feel the emotion, but recognize that this emotion is not all of his experience. Direct him to focus his attention on bodily sensations, sounds in the room and other sensory stimuli in the present. Trying to push the emotion away only tends to strengthen it, so have your client hold this emotion in mindfulness and with loving attention.

Continually bring your client's attention back to the sensations under your hands, to the flow of Reiki in the body – calming, soothing, quieting – while the emotion is still present. Remember that you are helping your client ride out the storm by connecting with the "calm beneath the storm," as Reiki anchors him into his body.

Allowing the strong emotion to arise, and to remain present with it, is a process of feeling and releasing the emotional pain stored in the body. Take as long as needed to restore balance, and then take time to process the experience with your client. Develop a plan and strategies to help your client increase his ability to be present with strong emotion in future sessions and also outside of sessions.

Emotional Dialogue

The purpose of this exercise is to explore and better

understand the nature of a troubling emotional symptom. As you apply Reiki, have your client consciously connect to the field of Ki and the flow of Reiki passing through her. Encourage her to rest and relax in the awareness of presence, and when she is ready, have her bring forward an emotion that is troubling or bring to mind a relationship, situation or belief that arouses strong emotion. While she practices remaining grounded, have your client try to immerse herself in this emotion and let it be as big as it wants to be. Now have her locate this emotion in her body and describe it.

Asking her the following questions can help guide her toward intuitive connection with this emotion:

- *Where does this emotion reside in the body?*
- *What does it feel like?*
- *What shape does it have? What color is it?*
- *What texture is it? Is it light and airy or dark and dense?*
- *Does it move around a lot or is it stationary?*
- *How old is it? How long has it been there?*
- *Can you increase its size?*
- *Can you reduce it by letting go in some way?*

Once she has established a basic connection with the emotion, she can then try asking herself questions about its function:

- *What kinds of situations elicit this emotion?*

- *What does this emotion do for me?*

- *How is it helping or protecting me?*

- *What is it helping me avoid?*

- *What is its origin?*

- *Is there a symbolic representation of this emotion?*

- *Is there an image or a picture?*

If the emotion exists in response to a certain situation or belief, help your client look at this situation from the perspective of the emotion (Brach, 2012). If, for example, the emotion is fear, have your client give the fear a voice and then ask her the following questions:

- *What is your fear trying to tell you? What is its mission?*

- *What does it believe is going to happen? What does it think would happen if you ignored it?*

- *What does it believe about you, about your life?*

- *Feel that you are inside the fear and sense how it is experiencing the world.*

- *What does the fear need from you?*

- *Is there anything in particular the fear wants to say to you?*

- *Is there anything you want to say to the fear?*

The information that you and your client obtain is helpful in deciding a direction for treatment. For instance, can you best work with this emotion by increasing clarity and insight, by accepting it and allowing it to be, by modifying beliefs that support it, by letting it go, or by creating affirmations that promote healing?

Mental-Emotional Release Technique

A technique that is helpful for releasing strong emotion is the Mental-Emotional Release Technique, adapted from the Emotional Release Therapy process developed by Walter Weston (1998). To begin, have your client lie on his back on the massage table. Next, instruct your client to choose a color that he is to imagine will be radiating from your palms during the treatment. There is no therapeutic significance to the color he chooses; any color is fine. Place your hands on the client's heart and solar plexus chakras, and begin giving Reiki. The heart chakra is the emotional center and the solar plexus is an energy center relating to the mind and mental activity, hence the name "Mental-Emotional."

Instruct your client to bring to mind a troubling memory, thought, or feeling that causes intense emotion. As memory and feeling come up, ask the client to send these reactions into your hands. You will feel heat coming into your hands as your client does this, and he will sense that the color under your hands is beginning to fade to white; this is an indicator that release is occurring. You can periodically "shake off" the energy he is sending into your hands, and then continue to give Reiki to the two chakras.

At times as a release is progressing, the client may have

another memory or feeling come up and when this occurs, you should encourage him to send this new reaction into your hands. Usually after ten to twenty minutes, the client has released as much of the charge as he is able to in one session.

After discharging strong emotion, many people feel an energetic void where their troubling thoughts or feelings had been stored in the body, and it is important to give Reiki to fill this void. It may take repeated sessions to re-solve a serious traumatic memory, but often progress is noted after only one session.

CASE EXAMPLE

Susan had been in a serious car accident and was seeking therapy to get over the feelings of anxiety and panic she felt whenever she had to ride in a car or bus. She found herself easily triggered by upset-ting memories of the accident and stated that since the accident she had felt more uneasy and vulnerable in new or unfamiliar circumstances.

We tried the Mental-Emotional Release Tech-nique and over the course of six to eight sessions, she reported great improvement. During the course of these sessions, she had other, older traumatic memo-ries arise and it was clear that the car accident had triggered unresolved trauma of other types that were stored in her body and energy field. Reiki helped to identify, process and release these older traumas.

Deconditioning Anxiety

Anxiety is the brain's distant early warning system, and when it arises, it signals danger, prompts vigilance and gears the body up for fight, flight or freeze behavior. But before we launch the nukes or run for the hills, we need to stop, breathe deeply, and recognize that we are feeling anxious. If we turn our attention and understanding toward that emotion, nine times out of ten we will see that there is no real danger, that some stimulus in our present experience has reminded the brain's associational network of a past threat, danger or trauma. A quick assessment of the current situation will usually verify this.

However, this assessment alone is not likely to stop the anxiety and adrenalin coursing through our system. What is more likely to stop it is the introduction of a self-soothing practice like giving oneself Reiki, holding oneself in self-compassion, repeating a calming mantra or phrase, or directing a peaceful and loving attention toward the anxiety. These practices inhibit the brain's danger scanning mechanism and the mind's emergency focus attentional style. They calm down the body's stress response, activate the body's relaxation response, and bring us back from the reservoir of the past and into the present moment.

The reservoir of anxiety that we carry is commonly triggered by current environmental stimuli, but this stimuli is not usually the cause of the anxiety. The cause lies in the past, in our conditioning, and in the unreleased effects of previous fears, dangers and traumas. When anxiety is triggered and we turn toward it, allowing it to be present just as it is, it often begins to fade. It is the resistance to it that enables and intensifies it.

When a client feels anxious, she must allow herself to feel the emotion while giving herself Reiki (if she is attuned) or holding herself in kindness and compassion. She must try not to make a story out of why she might be feeling anxious, and not assign it meaning or attach it to some current circumstance. Help her to think of the anxiety as just an energy arising, an energy that will fade away of its own accord if it is not resisted. As she practices this approach, she will find that over time she is slowly draining the reservoir of anxiety that she carries, as evidenced by feeling less anxious less often.

Open Focus Exercise for Emotional Pain

This is an exercise based upon the attentional work of Les Fehmi (2007), and is for dissolving emotional or physical pain. Begin by having your client lie on his back on the massage table. While applying Reiki to the back of his head, have him focus his attention on a painful emotion (e.g., fear), and have him experience this as fully as possible. Next, have your client find the physical location or locations where the emotion is expressing itself in the body (e.g., stomach and chest).

Now have your client broaden his awareness, becoming aware of background as well as foreground. Have him access all of his senses simultaneously: seeing, feeling, hearing, smelling, and tasting, as well as the space that permeates and surrounds him. Direct him to pay attention to and experience the space around him and inside of his body. Have him imagine himself as a cloud of particles floating in and permeated by a vast space.

Encourage your client to move toward and relax into the painful emotion in his body (e.g., into the fear in his stomach and chest) while simultaneously staying open to all of his sensory experience and the space it floats in. Generally he will discover that the painful knot of emotion he is experiencing will begin to fade and dissolve, and he will feel the tension in his body relax (Fehmi, 2007).

When we are in intense emotional or physical pain, our attention narrows and goes into emergency mode. We fixate on our pain, and if or when it begins to recede, we are hypervigilant for signs of its return. As we broaden our awareness and open our attention to our total sensory experience, including the pain, we find that not only does the pain dissolve, but we are far more present, alert and alive.

Meditation Exercises

Thondup (1996) presents several simple but useful meditation exercises that can help clients who are working with emotional pain. Using these meditations during a Reiki session has a powerful effect and it gives clients a method for self-soothing when strong emotion arises.

• When a client is feeling burdened by stress, worry or emotional suffocation, have him visualize a place in nature with an expansive view – standing on a mountain top, sitting by the ocean or staring up at a night sky filled with stars – while you give him Reiki. Have the client "relax in the feeling of openness, free from boundaries and limitations" (Thondup, 1996, p. 47). This will calm the mind and soothe negative emotional states. This comforting image can be installed in the client's energy field with the Sei He Ki technique.

• When the client is suffering from deep sadness, have her acknowledge its presence and turn toward it rather than away from it. As you give her the supporting energy of Reiki, have her feel the full weight of her sadness briefly, enough to recognize, acknowledge and embrace it while remaining grounded. When we face the sadness, we can begin to let it go.

Next, have her visualize the sadness symbolically, such as a dark cloud of energy in her head, heart, stomach, or wherever she feels the most pain. The cloud can be dark and ominous, if that feels appropriate to the client. It might feel dense, heavy or pressure-inducing, or lighter but all-encompassing. Help the client find whatever image and symbolism help her to more deeply connect with the sadness.

When she has fully connected with this cloud and allowed herself to experience and acknowledge the sadness, instruct her to begin letting go of it. One way to start doing this is through releasing a large exhaling breath, imagining the energy of the cloud exiting out of her body. Instruct your client to allow all of the cloud to drift out and away from her body, while she continues to breathe and you continue to give Reiki. Have her feel the relief as she imagines the cloud of sadness leaving. Have her envision it slowly but steadily floating away, farther and farther into the distant sky. As it becomes smaller and farther away, have her hold the intention to increasingly lose connection with it.

Finally, at the outermost horizon, have her visualize the cloud completely disappearing. See if she can feel that she has lost all connection with the sadness. Have her notice the lack of tension in her body, the feeling of freedom and relaxation filling her. See if she notices that she feels lighter, and have her rest in that feeling (Thondup, 1996).

Although this exercise focuses on sadness, you can use this with your clients regarding any troubling emotion. This sadness exercise highlights a significant point, which is that when we allow ourselves to fully feel a strong emotion that is welling up inside us, then we can begin to work with it, make peace with it and release it. For most of us, the natural impulse is to try to push unpleasant feelings away. We fear that if we allow ourselves to feel them, they will intensify and engulf us. Often, the opposite effect occurs. When we try to push away and ignore unpleasant feelings, they grow stronger and the mind becomes preoccupied with fearful thoughts about them.

Creating a Space for Emotion to Exist

There are times and situations in which strong emotional reactions are simply not ready to be modified or released. One therapeutic approach you can use when your client is mired in a strong emotional reaction is to create a space in which the emotion can exist.

First, have your client connect as fully as he can to the feeling he is experiencing, while you give him Reiki. Then have your client broaden his perspective by taking a mental step back and seeing the universal in his suffering. Help him remember and recognize that he is not alone in his pain. Ask him to bring to mind other people, known or unknown, who are in similar circumstances and feeling similar emotions, and ask him to see his suffering in the "10,000 beings" (the Buddhist expression that means everyone).

Finally, have your client give the emotion that he and others are experiencing space to exist in, creating a spacious awareness around this pain that allows it to be. Have your client acknowledge it and meet it with compassion and loving kindness.

In the space of the heart, there is an openness and receptivity that holds our capacity for love, compassion, passion, serenity and peace.

CHAPTER 7

Working with the Heart

Of the body, mind, emotion and heart, the heart is the aspect of our being that most expresses our true nature or essence. The heart is the seat of love, joy, peace, gratitude, and compassion. While the mind compares, compartmentalizes and thrives on difference, the heart recognizes our common humanity and seeks connection through compassionate identification with others. While the mind separates, the heart closes the gap of separation.

There are resources in the heart that can ease the pain of the body and mind and reduce the symptoms that they produce. We tap into these resources when we apply Reiki with the intention and attention to enter the space of the heart and connect with its qualities. After all, Reiki energy is heart energy. While giving Reiki to the client's heart chakra, have her open her awareness to the sensations in her heart and notice what she feels.

• In the space of the heart, there is an openness and receptivity that holds our capacity for love, serenity, peace and well-being.

• The heart is expansive and can hold what the mind cannot. The heart makes room for all of life and life's problems.

• The heart has the strength to engage life's problems as they are and to meet them with love, tolerance and acceptance.

• The heart can see through the illusion of separation and experience the Oneness we all share. The contemporary spiritual teacher Adyashanti (2011) states that to experience Oneness is to experience absolute intimacy with everything.

• The heart recognizes the judgments, limitations and conditioning of the mind and extends compassion and loving-kindness toward it. The heart soothes the pain, turmoil and confusion of the mind.

Levine (2005) writes that the heart has "the power to forgive, the strength to love, the trust to look deeper into what limits us," and the capacity to soften and extend mercy (p. 7). It is the path to peace.

The following exercises are practices you can use with your clients to help them connect with the resources of the heart in order to help treat mental and emotional symptoms.

Connecting with the Heart Exercise

While applying Reiki to the client's heart, have her focus her attention on this chakra in the center of her chest. Have her imagine looking into the space of the heart and picturing a soft, luminous ball of emerald green light. Can she envision this light gently expanding and contracting with the breath? As she breathes into and out of this ball of green light, she may notice that it intensifies in strength and color.

Now, as she rests in the awareness of her heart, ask her to contemplate one of the heart's qualities that is meaningful to her. Have her bring to mind this quality and focus her attention on how it feels. For example, can she feel the energy of compassion? Compassion involves the recognition and "clear seeing" of suffering. It involves feelings of kindness for ourselves and for others when there is suffering, so that our natural desire to help and comfort arises. Compassion recognizes our shared human condition, flawed and fragile as it is, and seeks to connect us one to another (Neff, 2011).

Have your client relax and allow the feeling of compassion to arise within her. She can try to immerse herself in that quality and feel its emanation from her heart. It may help her to silently repeat the word "compassion" to herself in order to bring this state into her awareness and into her body's experience. With practice, this exercise will deepen her connection to her heart and will increase her capacity for empathic connection with others.

Self-Compassion

The ability to cultivate compassion not just for others but for ourselves is a defining quality of the heart and a powerful healing practice in working to reduce symptoms.

In her book *Self-Compassion: Stop Beating Yourself Up and Leave Insecurity Behind*, Kristin Neff (2011) describes and discusses three core components of the practice of self-compassion.

First, self-compassion requires mindfulness, that we recognize and hold our experience in balanced awareness rather than ignoring our pain or exaggerating it. To meet our symptoms with self-compassion first requires an awareness of the mental, emotional and behavioral patterns that cause us to suffer. Neff (2011) cites research that implicates self-criticism, feelings of inadequacy and the tendency to ruminate (a recurrent, intrusive and uncontrollable style of thinking) as centrally causal factors in the experience of anxiety and depression.

As Neff (2011) states, "When we feel totally flawed and incapable of handling life's challenges, we tend to shut down in response to feelings of fear and shame" (p. 110). Additionally, rumination about negative events from the past leads to depression, while rumination about potentially negative events in the future leads to anxiety.

Mindfulness allows us to recognize the problematic thoughts, emotions and behaviors that generate anxiety and depression. It allows us to see that these thoughts and emotions are not necessarily true. In the practice of self-compassion, we allow them to arise and float away without resistance. We don't fuel the fire by taking them to heart, and this allows us to face our suffering with greater equanimity. Still, as Neff (2011) points out, there are times when mindfulness alone is not enough to avoid getting trapped in depressed and anxious mind states, and in this case we need to actually try to soothe ourselves.

The second component of self-compassion is self-kindness, being gentle and understanding with ourselves. We must activate and hold an attitude of comforting and caring for ourselves in the face of experiencing our symptoms. We must extend the same loving-kindness to ourselves that we extend to others. For example, when a client sees himself as inadequate and feels shame, he can try to be gentle with himself and hold his pain in kindness, not anger. He then can see how his conditioning is affecting him.

The third component required of self-compassion is the recognition of our common humanity, feeling connected with others in an experience of life. When we see that all beings suffer, we see the universal in our symptoms, and we don't feel so alone. Neff (2011) writes, "We balance the dark energy of negative emotion with the bright energy of love and social connection. These feelings deactivate the body's threat system (fight or flight) and activate the attachment system, calming down the amygdala and ramping up the production of oxytocin" (p. 113).

Neff's (2011) research on self-compassion shows that self-compassionate people tend to be less anxious and depressed, to experience fewer negative emotions (fear, irritability, hostility or distress), and to ruminate less than those who lack self-compassion.

When one experiences the energy of Reiki, it becomes apparent that Reiki embodies the components of compassion. Reiki quiets the mind, calms the body and opens the heart. Teaching clients to utilize these components to work with their symptoms during a Reiki treatment is a powerful and effective approach to symptom reduction.

Self-Compassion Exercise

Have your client connect with the feeling and flow of Reiki in his body and energy field. Instruct him to rest in this awareness. Once he feels grounded and present, have him call forward a mental, emotional or physical symptom and hold this symptom in mindfulness. Encourage your client to open to this experience and allow it to be just as it is, with nonjudgmental acceptance.

Next, have your client notice where in his body he feels the symptom, as well as any fearful or painful reactions to it. Guide him to hold these reactions in loving-kindness, and have compassion for the pain he is experiencing. Help your client develop the perspective that his symptom or symptoms are not uniquely his, that others with similar problems and conditioning have similar painful thoughts and feelings. Encourage him to see that it is not *his* mind that is the problem, it is *the* mind. It is not *his* anxiety, it is anxiety. Our symptoms are part of our shared human condition.

Helping a client to see the universal in his suffering normalizes his suffering and encourages him to see it as a part of life and an experience shared by others. This recognition fosters interconnectedness and helps him to feel a part of something larger than himself.

Neff (2011) presents a meditation that is a soothing balm for clients to use when they are experiencing intense mental, emotional or physical pain. I often introduce this to clients and have them repeat this meditation silently to themselves during a difficult Reiki session:

This is a moment of suffering.
Suffering is a part of life.
May I be kind to myself in this moment.
May I give myself the compassion I need. (Neff, 2011, p. 119)

When the Heart Feels Blocked

When qualities of the heart like compassion are difficult to experience, it may be that the heart's energy is being obscured. As your client focuses attention on her heart, have her try to detect this feeling of obstruction, resistance or blockage and then ask that the nature of this blockage be revealed. Often this obstruction is caused by the mind's judgments, held trauma energy or unreleased emotional pain such as grief, fear, anger, hurt, pain or jealousy. These judgments and emotions create a kind of barrier to our experience of the heart. They are an "armoring" around the heart that needs attention and exploration.

As you apply Reiki to your client's heart chakra, you may perceive this armoring intuitively, or you may feel *byosen* sensations in your hands, from intense heat to vibration or pain. Conversely, you may feel coolness and an absence of sensation, not even the normal Reiki warmth. Either extreme may indicate energy blockage.

As you continue to apply Reiki to your client's heart chakra, have her open her attention to her inner experience. Guide her to pay attention to any thoughts, images, emotions or sensations that arise. Does she experience a felt-sense of this blockage? Does she feel a certain emotion welling up? Often this information provides clues as to the nature of the blockage.

Exploring the Armoring of the Heart

One practice for working with this armoring is to seek out where in the body we are holding mental and emotional pain and release it there. The belly and solar plexus are common areas for emotional holding, as they are sensitive sensing and diagnostic centers in the body (Sui, 2000). They frequently take in, hold and store the unreleased pain that obscures our capacity to feel love, joy, peace, compassion, and contentment. In response to life's painful experiences, we learn to hold our breath, contract our muscles, and tighten our bellies, and this muscular tension locks emotional pain in the body. We learn to physically brace ourselves against life and to guard ourselves against future loss and hardship.

We subsequently develop the capacity to "hold life out," to keep it at arm's length. As a result, our breathing and digestive functions become dysregulated and the belly becomes habitually hardened. The belly and the solar plexus are not the only areas of the body that accumulate unreleased pain, although they are the most common. Other areas include the back, shoulder blades, shoulders, neck and eyes.

We can begin to both explore and work with emotional armoring of the belly and solar plexus by using Reiki and breath work. The following exercise is an adaptation and extension of the soft belly meditation (Levine, 1987, 1991).

While simultaneously applying Reiki to your client's solar plexus and abdomen, encourage him to breathe slowly and evenly while paying attention to the rise and fall of the breath. As he breathes in, have him feel the way the breath gently expands his belly outward and into your hands. Now direct him to pay attention to any emotion, any feeling of resistance or holding, any reluctance to breathe in. Can he identify the nature of this emotional resistance? With the in-breath, have him allow this emotion to come forward and embrace it, and with the out-breath, have him soften, relax and release it.

Does this emotion feel like sadness or grief? Does he notice any feeling of fear or shame? Does he notice a feeling of vulnerability in the presence of certain judgments, memories or images from the past? While working with this exercise, have your client hold himself in an attitude of compassion and loving-kindness.

Examples of phrases that address emotion on the in-breath include:

- *Breathing in loneliness*
- *Breathing in shame*
- *Breathing in anger*

- *Breathing in fear*
- *Breathing in hurt*
- *Breathing in the fear of my childhood*
- *Breathing in the pain of my childhood*
- *Breathing in the loss of a normal childhood*

Examples of phrases that support release on the out-breath include:

- *Breathing out relief*
- *Breathing out release*
- *Breathing out peace*
- *Breathing out safety*
- *Breathing out compassion*

As mentioned, one of the ways that Reiki works is by releasing the energetic charge underlying stored emotion. This release may intensify the emotion before it eases, so it is important to inform your client of this possibility before you begin. Once your client has discharged all that he is likely to in this session, it is helpful to apply Reiki to his knees and feet for a few minutes to help ground and stabilize him. Often this exercise will generate clinical information to process, and with practice it will help your client to relax the emotional armoring around the heart and connect more easily with its resources.

Heartfulness

Heartfulness is the practice of reaching out to others, and to our own body and mind, from the spaciousness of our heart. It is the practice of relating to our problems with the resources that the heart can offer: peace, love, compassion, kindness, and forgiveness (Levine, 1987, 2005).

When we direct our attention toward the body and toward the mind from the spaciousness of the heart, our problems and our pain become more workable. When we meet our grief with the energy of the heart, we feel compassion for ourselves. Heartfulness is a practice in which we see the mind's struggle and we hold this struggle in the loving embrace of the heart. This practice develops our ability to be present with ourselves in more loving and self-accepting ways.

A Heartfulness Approach to the Mind

To work on the egoic mind from a heartfulness perspective, try the following exercise with your client (Levine, 1987).

1. Instruct your client to connect with the awareness that seems to be located in her head and looks out at the world through her eyes.

2. Have her gently allow this awareness to sink down into the space of her heart chakra and imagine that she is looking out at the world from this space. She may notice that she is feeling a more expanded state of awareness and that her peripheral vision has increased.

3. From this heart-centered state of awareness, have her imagine that she can look up and see the egoic mind at work. Have her imagine that she is able to observe how

the mind is thinking and what it is thinking about. Explain to her that from this vantage point she is relating *to* the egoic mind and not *from* it, as we usually do.

When our awareness and attention rest in the physical space of our heart, we create distance from the mind. We move into a perceptual state of mindfulness from which it is easier to witness the mind's movements. This disengagement enables us to have empathy for the mind's conditioning, to send loving-kindness to it in order to ease its judgments and pain and to help it to heal.

Heartfulness has the ability to alter the mind's functioning by softening its judgments, opinions and perceptions. It can slow the ego's steady stream of thought production and "open its eyes" to a kinder, more accepting view of itself and others. Heartfulness allows the body to relax, to breath more deeply, to feel more peaceful and to be more present.

Exercise for Letting the Mind Float in the Space of the Heart

Have your client bring a negative self-statement, belief or unacceptable thought to mind while you apply Reiki. For example, she can bring forth a belief such as, "I'm not enough," "I'm such a loser," or "I'm undeserving of love," or a judgment toward others or toward the world at large such as, "People are not trustworthy," "People are just out for themselves," or "The world is a dangerous place." Have your client try to experience this belief or judgment as fully as she can.

As you focus Reiki on her heart chakra, instruct the client to allow this belief to settle into that space in the center of her chest. She can visualize bringing the belief from the mind down into her heart chakra, allowing it to become enveloped by the healing energy of the heart. Have her allow the belief to just reside there in the spaciousness of the heart. Now ask the client to describe how her heart experiences the belief or judgment.

Because the heart can see the distortion in our thoughts, this exercise begins to soften our beliefs and judgments. It enables us to see where these thoughts came from and the conditioning they grew out of. "Clear seeing" allows us the opportunity to challenge the veracity of our thoughts and to modify them when needed.

*The body, mind, emotion and heart are as powerful as the sun,
but can be blocked or eclipsed by the held energy and "shadow" of
relationship trauma.*

CHAPTER 8

Working with the Held Energy of Relationship Trauma

Many people carry around the toxic effects of past and present relationship trauma without realizing it. These effects are experienced in different ways in the body and in the H.E.F. For instance, they can express as an energy block, an energy cord, a feeling of presence around a person, intrusive thoughts, ideas or memories, or emotions of anxiety, sadness, hurt, shame or anger.

One way to work with this toxicity is to have the client bring the image of the toxic person to mind and have him notice where and how he holds this energy in his body or energy field. Common places for energy storage include the forehead, solar plexus, chest, throat, abdomen, or in the field around their body. Once you and the client have found the location and have a description of what this held energy feels like, then you can use Reiki to release it.

Aura Clearing and Sweeping

For those practitioners who have taken Advanced Reiki

Training from the International Center for Reiki Training, the aura clearing technique is an excellent method for releasing held trauma energy. Aura clearing has several steps. First, the practitioner helps the client locate, connect to and describe an energy cord or energy block while giving her Reiki. Second, the practitioner uses Reiki to remove the energy cord or block by pulling the negative energy out and releasing it. Once the block has been removed, the practitioner fills the area with Reiki and seals it with the power symbol. For more detailed information on the aura clearing technique, please refer to Rand's (2003) *Reiki Master Manual: Advanced Reiki Training*.

Another approach to aura clearing is the sweeping technique used by Sui (1990) and discussed earlier in this book in Chapter 4. Sweeping can be used to break the energetic connection between the client and the toxic person. To do this, work with the client to find the location of the energy connection on his body and then sweep your hands through this area twenty-five to thirty times. When you both feel the energetic connection has been broken, apply Reiki to the affected area.

After any energy removal it is important to fill the released or vacated area with Reiki and to install corrective thoughts and feelings if appropriate. You can draw the mental-emotional and power symbol over the area to "seal" in the corrective thoughts and feelings.

CASE EXAMPLES

One client felt an energetic sensation in the energy field next to her throat and shoulder on the right side of her body. This energy felt cold, and sinister. The process of aura clearing brought out unpleasant memories and scenes from childhood. These scenes led us to talk about the negative messages she grew up with and the way these messages were still at work within her. We worked to remove the negative energy using release techniques and then installed corrective messages.

Another client experienced a black cloud of energy above her shoulders, neck and back, which she described as a "creepy feeling." She associated this feeling with being sexually objectified by her father throughout her childhood and adolescence, although she had no memory of being physically sexually abused. I used aura clearing, with sweeping and cord cutting (slicing through the energy cord above the client's body with a karate-like chop of the practitioner's hand), every session for many weeks and eventually this cloud dissipated. Throughout this process, memories would surface and fade away as she released negative energy.

Removing an Energetic Block or Healing an Energetic Wound

The following discussion, exercise and case example are written by Vanessa L. Vlahakis, a mental health counselor, Reiki Master Teacher and psychic medium who utilizes Psychotherapeutic Reiki techniques in her private practice (*www.evolvingsouls.us*). In a personal communication with me, Vanessa discussed an exercise she and a client used to treat an energy blockage that expresses a very creative and thoughtful perspective, and a useful approach to working with relationship traumas.

Vanessa writes:

> In the course of my work, I've found that the held energy of a traumatic experience or relationship can express itself either as a symbolic "block" to be removed, or a "wound" to be healed. There are several steps to working with and clearing or healing energy blocks and wounds. Begin by asking for guidance from both your spiritual team and your client's spiritual team so that effective healing for the highest good of all takes place in the session. Psychotherapeutic Reiki sessions are always a balance between intuition and therapeutic training, between trusting spiritual guidance and trusting yourself. Know that if you set clear intentions, you will be guided to do what is right for both you and your client.
>
> While your client is on her back on the table, give Reiki to her crown for a few minutes to begin the flow of energy. Have her close her eyes and take a few deep breaths to help her center, relax

and settle into the experience. When she is ready, help her locate and describe the symbolic energy block or wound she is experiencing. This could be a representation of an emotion, memory, past trauma, difficult relationship or current situation. She can use the bullet-pointed, exploratory questions outlined in Chapters 3, 5 and 6 of this book to help her connect with and identify the location, shape, size, texture, weight, and deeper meaning of the energetic block or wound.

Once that is accomplished, the next step is to have your client connect intuitively and emotionally with this held energy blockage while you give Reiki to the identified location, so that she can dialogue with it. You may receive intuitive information as well, but it is important to allow her to try and connect with the blockage herself first. Giving your client the space to open up and receive guidance is a way to honor her intuition and inherent ability to heal herself. It is also empowering for her to realize all the wisdom she needs to heal is within.

Your client can have this dialogue out loud or silently in her head, if that is more comfortable for her. If she is truly struggling to connect with the energetic blockage, you can offer some of your intuitive information and that may help her connect. Sometimes I will move back to the client's crown and third eye chakras for a brief period, as the Reiki can help open up those chakras if the client is struggling to connect intuitively.

Questions to facilitate the connection could include:

- *What do you feel as you look at the energetic block/*

wound?

- *Do you know why it is here, what its purpose is?*
- *Can you sense what it needs from you right now?*
- *Is there anything it wants to say to you?*
- *What are its fears and concerns?*
- *What do you want to say to it?*
- *Does it feel ready to go? Has it served its purpose?*

More often than not, energetic blocks and wounds have formed from past or recent traumas and now exist as a form of "protection" against future similar traumas. The subconscious belief is that if the block or wound can prevent a client from fully connecting to or experiencing a similar situation, she won't be vulnerable to the pain she experienced the first time. Though this "protection" is misguided, it needs to be respected as a psychological, emotional and energetic survival method.

As such, energetic blocks and wounds always need to be recognized and honored as parts of a client that need a voice. It is important to approach these held energy blockages with compassion and acceptance, rather than anger or frustration. I have found that when the block or wound is acknowledged as a deeper part of the client that needs to express its purpose, fears and concerns, it becomes ready to be released. Once the client begins a dialogue with this part and assures the blockage that its function is recognized and appreciated, and that she no longer needs its "protection," it usually releases its hold.

After the intuitive connection and dialogue have taken place, both you and the client can assess and determine whether it is a block that needs to be removed and released, or a wound that needs to be moved and healed. The continued Reiki from the practitioner helps to energetically lubricate the area for either case. Most often, the held energy blockage will intuitively "tell" you what needs to happen; trust what you both receive.

If it is to be removed, you can use Rand's (2003) aura clearing technique to pull out the unneeded energy from the client's body. Once you are holding the symbolic energy block in your hands, remember to thank it for its service, and encourage it to go into the light to be transmuted. You may toss the energy up and away from the client, and it will go where it needs to; your guides and other spiritual helpers will see to this.

Sometimes held energy blockages need to be transformed through the energy of the heart rather than removed and released. This is particularly empowering for the client, as she is now in charge of healing her own wound rather than having the practitioner "remove" it. It highlights the immense capacity of the heart's energy to heal and transmute even deeply entrenched traumas, and enforces the idea that the client always has the power within to heal herself.

If this is the case, have the client continue her intuitive connection with the wound and encourage it to move from its current location toward the heart chakra. You can support this by beaming Reiki to the area of the wound and gently sweeping your hands toward the heart chakra, as if to sweep the wound toward the desired location. The flowing Reiki will facilitate the energetic move. Follow your intuition to sense when the blockage has completed its move; most likely, the client will know when it is done. Allow her to guide the process and inform you when she feels it has been accomplished.

In either case, once the block has been removed or the wound has been moved, fill the vacated area with Reiki and seal it with the mental-emotional and power symbols. You and the client may come up with an affirmation to install in the area, or you may choose to just fill it with Reiki. You will know intuitively when it is "full" and you can seal it with the mental-emotional and power symbols. If the wound was moved to the heart chakra, give Reiki to that area as well to help facilitate the transmutation.

Follow your intuition about what the client needs at this time to process and integrate what has happened, but be sure to incorporate her own intuitive knowledge about what she needs. The session is a partnership between you both, and if you respect that process throughout, it will be a very successful session.

Vanessa's Case Example

Maria came to me with an energetic wound on her solar plexus chakra that represented a self-worth injury of believing she was never "good enough." When she intuitively connected to it, she saw a symbolic black metal claw with a large flat center and five or six long pointed legs, clamped around her solar plexus chakra. Energetic roots extended from the center of the claw down into the chakra, and the long pointy legs wrapped around the chakra. It was a fairly scary looking symbolic blockage.

Initially, we both believed it needed to be removed. Once Maria established a dialogue with it, she realized the block was in fact a wounded part of her that was terrified of being separated from her, and just wanted to be held and accepted. We determined it wanted to be moved up into the heart chakra to be healed and transmuted, so we changed the direction of our work.

As Maria mentally dialogued with the wound, I beamed Reiki into her solar plexus chakra to soften the claw's hold. Soon, I intuitively saw its energetic roots begin to dissolve in the healing Reiki energy. We then both independently got intuitive images of the symbolic claw slowly starting to climb up Maria's body from her solar plexus toward her heart chakra. I beamed Reiki and slowly motioned my hands toward the heart, envisioning the Reiki carrying the claw like a gentle wave.

When the claw reached the heart chakra, it sank into the healing energy slowly, like an object sinking into a can of paint. The loving energy enveloped and permeated the claw, and Maria soon saw it transform from black angled metal into a delicate crystal snowflake. She immediately felt light and free, and we could both feel the snowflake's joy at being healed.

This was a powerful experience which taught me that not all held energy blockages need to be treated as "bad energy" to be removed. Sometimes, they deserve to stay with us and be transformed and healed. Maria felt empowered because she was able to heal her own self-worth issue, and symbolically re-parent the wound so that it could transform into something healthy and beautiful.

It is conceivable that energetic wounds might want to be healed in a chakra other than the heart. A wound of disempowerment might want to be placed into the solar plexus chakra to be bathed in the energy of worth and personal power. A wound from being silenced might benefit from being placed in the throat chakra to heal in the energy of speaking one's truth. As with most of this work, it is always important to listen to the intuition both you and your client are receiving. The Reiki energy will let you know what needs to happen, and if that is honored, great healing can take place.

Inner Child Rescue

This is a technique for helping an adult resolve the effects of an interpersonal trauma from childhood. The first step is to have the client bring up and describe the dysfunctional childhood situation scene by scene while you give Reiki to the back of her head. Encourage the client to be as specific as possible and to re-experience the emotions she felt back then, while remaining grounded.

The second step is to "rewrite" history and create a happy ending. In this step, you and your client construct a functional scene to replace the dysfunctional one. For example, if in the actual event the client was beaten, in the functional scene the beating is prevented or stopped by a healthy caretaker who steps in and protects the child. The purpose of this second task is to right the wrong of the original trauma.

The third step is to install the corrective scene into the client's energy field. This can be done using the Sei He Ki technique or by placing one hand on the client's solar plexus chakra and the other on her heart chakra. I have found both formats to be effective. In this step, have the client recall the dysfunctional scene and then, while giving Reiki, present the corrective scene out loud while the client visualizes this and takes it in. Set the intention for the corrective scene to be installed and set into the client's energy field, and seal it with the power symbol.

Case Example

Debby lived with a recurrent and intrusive memory of a childhood incident with her father, who was an angry and abusive man. Debby was about thirteen years old when she did something to upset her father. Her father responded by grabbing her, pulling down her pants and spanking her in front of her mother and sister while yelling at her and belittling her. Debby was humiliated and flooded with shame by this incident, and as she grew older she continued to relive this incident repeatedly in her mind.

The corrective scene we installed involved a woman neighbor whom Debby liked and trusted rushing through the door while the father was starting to spank her, pushing the father away and helping her get dressed. Then the neighbor sat the parents down and yelled at them and told them they would never treat Debby this way again. The reason Debby didn't have her mother intervene in this corrective scene is that Debby knew her mother was ineffective in standing up to her father, so that scenario wouldn't be realistic and would not have worked.

Debby found that the inner child rescue helped to remove the emotional charge from the memory, and as time went by she found herself thinking less about the incident.

Forgiveness Exercise

Another technique that is helpful in breaking an energetic tie to another person is a forgiveness exercise discussed by Levine (1987). While giving the client Reiki, have him bring to mind a person who has caused him harm, as well as the harmful incident itself. While giving the client Reiki, have him silently speak to this person and repeat the following: "For the harm you have caused me by your thoughts, your words, your actions, I forgive you now." The client continues to repeat this phrase throughout the session until he feels forgiveness arising within himself.

The client may also use this technique to ask for forgiveness by repeating the following: "For any harm I may have caused you by my thoughts, my words, my actions, I ask for forgiveness now." This is a simple but powerful technique for releasing the charge around any unhealed relationship and it often promotes a sense of closure or resolution within the client.

Treatment templates offer ways to bring Reiki to the physical, mental, emotional and relational aspects of a problem.

CHAPTER 9

Treatment Templates for Various Psychological Problems

The following templates were created from the concepts and techniques discussed in this book, and my personal treatment experiences using the Psychotherapeutic Reiki model. These templates offer ways to combine different treatment techniques with the physical, mental, emotional and relational aspects of a problem.

Stress, Irritability, Anxiety and Grief

Negative conditioning, unreleased emotion and unresolved trauma keep the body stuck in the stress mode. Stress reactions are characterized by symptoms of fight, flight and freeze behavior in the face of a specific stressor. Anxiety and grief are energetically similar to stress, share many of the same causes and symptoms, and are thus included in this treatment template.

Stress reactions are a normal response to a threatening, overwhelming or unintegratable stimulus. They have a beginning, a middle and an end, but become more complicated when stress is repetitive and when their symptoms are not released or cleared. In acute reactions the stressor is clear and identifiable, but in cases of chronic stress the individual has been conditioned to respond symptomatically to even minor stressors that may be difficult to identify, as is typical in many cases of generalized anxiety disorder.

The fight mode can be triggered by fear and is characterized by irritability and anger, angry thoughts, and defensive or aggressive impulses and behaviors. In fight mode, we are generally short-tempered, intolerant and tense. In this mode our energy level may be high, but it usually converts to fatigue when the stressful event has passed and the adrenaline wears off. Normal examples of this mode are commonly experienced while driving and encountering other drivers on the road.

The flight mode is characterized by heightened anxiety and a strong desire to avoid or withdraw from a stressful situation. Thoughts are generally fear-based, can be irrational and may be catastrophically expectant. Normal examples of this mode are commonly experienced when faced with the task of public speaking.

The freeze mode is characterized by confusion and an inability to act, feel or think clearly. In freeze mode we may feel dissociation, a sense of unreality and/or disconnection from the body, or that time is standing still. There is often an intense desire to hide or try to become invisible. Normal examples of this mode are commonly experienced when we come face-to-face with a stressor we can neither oppose nor escape, such as being confronted by an employer.

Common to all three modes are various degrees of emotional flooding, hyperarousal and muscular tension.

In all three modes, people often find themselves breathing shallowly or holding their breath; breath dysregulation increases anxiety and decreases energy. Many people experiencing stress reactions have a combination of symptoms from all three modes, but others may be chronically polarized in one particular mode.

Developing a treatment plan for symptoms of stress, anxiety or grief begins with an assessment of how symptoms are expressing in the mind, emotion and body. Because these components are all part of an interactive system, you can begin treatment in any one component, and change in one will bring about change in the others. I have found it most effective to combine "talk and touch." While the client and I talk about a particular problem or are using a specific treatment technique, I give Reiki to the client's body using the key hand placements that relate to the chakra(s) and problem on which we are focusing. (Please refer to Chapter 1 for a list of chakras and their related issues and functions.)

Treating the mind usually revolves around belief work and/or creating and installing corrective affirmations and beliefs. In assessing the mind, first identify specific problematic thoughts and beliefs (e.g., "The world is a dangerous place," "I can't cope," or "I'm so inadequate"). Then help your client assess the validity and truthfulness of these beliefs as they pertain to the present day. A current belief may have been true in childhood but it isn't true now, or perhaps it's only partly true now. Challenging people's beliefs may threaten their identity and thus arouse strong emotion, defensiveness and resistance. Enter into this examination gently and in a non-blaming and supportive manner. (If you need to put the blame somewhere, blame the client's conditioning and not them.)

After you and your client have identified several core beliefs and are working towards modifying these, the next step is to construct corrective thoughts and beliefs that counter them (e.g., "My world is safe enough today," "I have resources to draw upon for help with my problems," "I'm a capable person," or "I'm good enough"). These corrective beliefs are used as affirmations which can be installed in the energy centers of the body during the hands-on Reiki treatment.

In assessing the emotional aspects of the problem, help your client identify the specific emotions involved. Treatment for emotional distress usually involves the use of one of two approaches: either accepting and practicing presence with emotional pain that can't be released (*letting it be*), or using techniques that release the pain that can be released (*letting it go*).

To help treat unresolved emotional pain, use one of the release techniques discussed in this book, or have your client bring up and hold a painful emotion throughout the treatment while both you and your client hold the intention for that emotion to be healed. This allows the Reiki to help release the energetic charge underlying it. Release techniques can be difficult for clients so it is important to train them in the use of emotional regulation skills and grounding. During the treatment, closely monitor your client's comfort level and instruct her to signal if the emotional pain becomes too intense.

The body and energy field store and carry the mental and emotional aspects of the client's stress, anxiety and grief. If you and your client have identified certain bodily locations and areas of holding (energy blockages), you can treat these areas directly with Reiki as outlined. However, there are key hand placements to use for treating stress, irritability, anxiety and grief. You can give a Reiki treatment using just these positions or you can incorporate them into a whole-body treatment.

While your client is lying on her back, the key hand placements are the back of the head, crown of the head, ears, forehead (third eye chakra), eyes and throat chakra, and the front solar plexus and front heart chakras. Then have your client turn over and treat the back solar plexus chakra (the Meng Mein), the back of the heart chakra, the root chakra and the feet.

Treat the key hand placements with Reiki for at least three or five minutes per position. If you are drawn to stay longer, certainly do so, especially if the *byosen* is strong and your hands are very warm, tingly, vibrating or feeling pain. These are all signs that the Reiki is working to clear a blockage. If the *byosen* is particularly strong, try sweeping your hands twenty-five to fifty times above the body and through the chakra(s), and draw the power symbol over the chakra(s) after sweeping. As you move through the series of hand placements, you and your client can also install an affirmation by silently repeating this affirmation to yourselves.

The client's participation is enhanced by her use of positive intention, directed attention, breath work and creative visualization. When you direct your client's attention toward the areas of the body you are working on, it enhances energy flow ("Where thought goes, energy flows"). Having her breathe slowly, deeply and evenly assists the flow of Reiki and calms body and mind.

Sui (2000) suggests a positive visual exercise for your client to use during a Reiki treatment for stress or anxiety:

> Visualize the stressful condition. Look at it detachedly and objectively. Visualize that you are calm and doing the right thing. *By doing this you are creating a positive thought pattern that will condition you to react positively to the stressful condition.* What we call stress is our negative reaction to a taxing situation. Do abdominal breathing when doing positive self-imagining. (p. 60)

Phobias and Fears

A phobia is an uncontrollable, dysregulated fear that is carried in the solar plexus, throat and crown chakras (Sui, 2000). To treat specific fears, assess and define mental and emotional targets with the corresponding bodily locations, and apply techniques from the Four Therapeutic Tasks. Invite the client's participation with the use of directed attention, breath work and visualization.

With your client lying on his back, the key hand placements are the crown of the head, ears, forehead (third eye chakra), eyes, and the throat and front solar plexus chakras. Have your client turn over and treat the back heart chakra and the back solar plexus chakra (the Meng Mein). As discussed previously, spend three to five minutes per placement but feel free to let your guidance and intuition determine the length of treatment and other hand placements to use. (On occasion I have spent up to one half hour on one hand placement.)

Obsessive Thoughts and Compulsive Behaviors

The treatment for obsessive, unwanted and distressing thoughts as well as for compulsive and repetitive behavior utilizes the same hand placements as outlined in treating phobias and fears; on the front of the body, the crown of the head, ears, forehead (third eye chakra), eyes, and the throat and solar plexus chakras, and on the back of the body, the heart and solar plexus chakras. These energy centers are common sites for the collection of negative thought energy.

In concert with the treatment of the body, focusing attention on belief work and specifically on modifying the mind's obsessive thoughts can be quite useful. For example, while the client is holding an obsessive thought, simultaneously have her direct her attention to the body, the breath and the feeling of Reiki. Follow these steps by installing positive, corrective thoughts and affirmations as described in Chapter 5.

Depression

Psychological depression is related to the experience of loss, so it is important to get a good history of the kinds of losses your client has suffered. Grief is a normal reaction to the loss of a loved one, but it can turn into depression when grieving is unattended, interrupted or protracted.

Depression can also result from a perceived loss of control over one's life due to trauma, the loss of a way of life, a lost opportunity, the loss of health or a loss of hope for the future. The mentality of victimhood can become second-nature to those who have suffered repeated losses and traumas, and rumination of negative cognitive constructs forms a feedback loop that constantly reinforces the depression. Your client may present with multiple losses and causes for the depression, but for this approach you need to start with one identifiable loss and a related set of beliefs or emotions to target.

Use the same preparatory steps as indicated in the previous templates. Help your client to identify and describe a specific loss with accompanying thoughts, emotions and body location. While your client is laying on his back, the key hand placements are the crown chakra, back of the head, ears, eyes, forehead (third eye chakra), solar plexus chakra, spleen (left side under the rib cage), sacral chakra and the palms of his hands. Have your client turn over and treat the back of his head again, the back heart chakra and the root chakra, and finish by treating the soles of his feet. As with the previous templates, work with mental and emotional issues during the course of the body treatment.

CASE EXAMPLE

Marsha was seeking help for symptoms of social anxiety. She indicated that encounters with others, especially people she needed help from, or people in a position of authority over her, made her nervous and "stressed." While interacting with someone she would become self-conscious, nervous and preoccupied with how she was coming across. These worries often interfered with her ability to express herself, which made her feel self-critical and stupid and led her to wonder how she was being perceived. She always imagined the other person was critically judging her.

There were several different ways that we used talk therapy and Reiki to work on this problem over the course of several years. Initially, I helped Marsha experience the calming effects of Reiki and develop the anchors she needed to feel more grounded in her body. I taught her to use self-monitoring processes, breath work and emotional regulation skills. I attuned Marsha to Reiki Level One so she could use Reiki on herself between sessions.

We developed targets and critical incidents to work with in the following ways:

1. While Marsha was receiving Reiki, I had her focus her attention on various scenarios that activated her symptoms. For example, she brought up a recent anxiety-provoking meeting she had with her supervisor. We worked on the thoughts and related beliefs she had during their interchange. In later sessions we used some of this information to install corrective thoughts.

2. During Reiki sessions I had Marsha bring to mind critical incidents and direct her attention toward her emotional state. She discovered that what she called "stress" and nervousness were more accurately anxiety, fear of criticism, rejection and shame at feeling inadequate. These emotions were rooted in childhood familial patterns.

As we explored where these emotions lived in her body, Marsha noticed the way her body carried tension. She became flushed and held her breath when feeling emotionally flooded. Over time, as Marsha began to feel more tolerant and accepting of her emotions, she emptied the "well" of pain that she carried. We used Practicing Presence and Releasing and Clearing techniques to reduce emotional intensity and promote emotional acceptance.

3. During Reiki sessions, we investigated childhood events and interactions that contributed to her

symptoms of social anxiety. This investigation provided us with additional targets to work on.

4. Some sessions were focused on installing corrective thoughts and behaviors. For example, we would construct potentially triggering situations, and while Marsha held herself with greater self-compassion she would visualize herself handling these situations successfully and with empowerment.

Over time, Marsha healed and released issues of social anxiety while increasing interpersonal tolerance.

Concluding Remarks

Psychotherapeutic Reiki is an approach to therapy that looks at clients and their symptoms from the perspective of subtle energy, or Ki. The use of Reiki in this approach is not meant to be a substitute for traditional talk therapy, but rather an adjunct to it. Whereas in traditional talk therapy we are trying to modify and reduce symptoms on the mental, emotional and behavioral levels of the Human Energy Field, in this approach we are extending this modification to the subtle energy level as well. This is the level of the H.E.F. in which most psychological symptoms originate or are maintained, and consequently this is a necessary and effective level on which to intervene.

The interventions that I have presented in this book are interventions that I either took and adapted from others or have created in order to modify the flow and balance of Ki energy for the purposes of symptom reduction. These interventions suggested themselves from the work my clients and I have created together. If the reader found a theoretical perspective or technique in this book particularly interesting or useful, I encourage her to read the original source or sources referenced for more depth and to fully experience and work with this perspective.

I invite practitioners of this approach to find and create new treatment techniques that suit their style of working so that new interventions will emerge as this work continues. It is my hope that this book will encourage other clinicians to learn Reiki and integrate its healing potential into their practices.

Index of Techniques

Appendix A

IARP Reiki Code of Ethics*

1. Abide by a vow of confidentiality. Any information that is discussed within the context of a Reiki session is confidential between the client and the practitioner.

2. Provide a safe and comfortable area for sessions or classes and work to provide an empowering and supportive environment for clients and students.

3. Always treat clients and students with the utmost respect and honor.

4. Have a pure and clear intention to offer your services for the highest healing good of the client and highest potential of the student.

5. Provide a brief oral or written description of what happens during a session and what to expect before a client's initial session. Provide a clear written description of subjects to be taught during each level of Reiki prior to class and list what the student will be able to do after taking the class.

6. Be respectful of others' Reiki views and paths.

7. Educate clients/students on the value of Reiki and explain that sessions do not guarantee a cure, nor are they a

*Source: *www.iarp.org/iarp-code-ethics*

substitute for qualified medical or professional care. Reiki is one part of an integrative healing or wellness program.

8. Suggest a consultation or referral for clients to qualified licensed professionals (medical doctor, licensed therapist, etc.) when appropriate.

9. Never diagnose or prescribe. Never suggest that the client/student change prescribed treatment or interfere with the treatment of a licensed health care provider.

10. Be sensitive to the boundary needs of individual clients and students.

11. Never ask clients to disrobe (unless in the context of a licensed massage therapy session at the client's option). Do not touch the genital area or breasts. Practice hands-off healing of these areas if treatment is needed.

12. Be working to create harmony and friendly cooperation between Reiki Practitioners/Master Teachers in the community and represent IARP in the most professional manner.

13. Act as a beacon in your community by doing the best job possible.

14. Work to empower your students to heal themselves and to encourage and assist them in the development of their work with Reiki or their Reiki practices.

15. Be actively working on your own healing so as to embody and fully express the essence of Reiki in everything that you do.

Appendix B

Informed Consent Form

I, _____, understand that Reiki sessions are given for the purpose of stress reduction, relaxation and as an aide to balancing my energy field and possibly improving my general wellness.

I understand that Reiki treatment is not a substitute for medical treatment, medication or diagnosis and that Reiki practitioners do not interfere with the treatment of a licensed medical professional. It is recommended that I concurrently work with my doctor or medical specialist for any medical condition(s) I may have.

I understand that prior to my first Reiki session, I will receive an explanation and description of a Reiki treatment and the procedures used; I have the right to have any and all of my questions answered to the best of my practitioner's ability.

I understand that except for taking off my shoes, I remain fully clothed during a Reiki session.

I understand that Reiki practitioners do not touch breasts or genital areas of the body and that I have the right to refuse or terminate, at any time, any touch on any part of my body.

I understand that Reiki and touch therapy can evoke strong emotions, sensations and memories, and agree that if I experience discomfort during the session, I will communicate this to the practitioner so that these issues can be addressed.

_____

CLIENT SIGNATURE   DATE

_____

PRACTITIONER SIGNATURE   DATE

References and Bibliography

Achterberg, J., Dossey, B., & Kolkmeier, L. (1994). *Rituals of healing: Using imagery for health and wellness.* New York, NY: Bantam Books.

Adyashanti (Producer). (2011). *Video Satsang with Adyashanti: Intimacy with everything (Vol. 61)* [DVD]. Palo Alto, CA: Open Gate Publishing.

Benjamin, B. E., & Sohnen-Moe, C. (2003). *The ethics of touch.* Tucson, AZ: Sohnen-Moe Associates, Inc.

Borysenko, J. (1987). *Minding the body, mending the mind.* Reading, MA: Addison-Wesley Pub. Co. Inc.

Brach, T. (2012). *True refuge: Finding peace and freedom in your own awakened heart.* New York, NY: Bantam Books.

Brennan, B. (1993). *Light emerging: The journey of personal healing.* New York, NY: Bantam Books.

Caudill, M. A. (2009). *Managing pain before it manages you* (3rd ed.). New York, NY: Gilford Publications.

Cohen, D. (2000). *Finding a joyful life in the heart of pain.* Boston, MA: Shambhala Publications, Inc.

Fehmi, L., & Robbins, J. (2007). *The open-focus brain: Harnessing the power of attention to heal mind and body.* Boston, MA: Trumpeter Books.

Feinstein, D., Eden, D., & Craig, G. (2005). *The promise of energy psychology: Revolutionary tools for dramatic personal change.* New York, NY: The Penguin Group.

Germer, C. K., Siegel, R. D., & Fulton, P. R. (Eds.). (2005). *Mindfulness and psychotherapy*. New York, NY: Guilford Press.

Gleisner, E. F. (1992). *Reiki in everyday living*. Laytonville, CA: White Feather Press.

Hanh, T. N. (1991). *Peace is every step: The path of mindfulness in everyday life*. New York, NY: Bantam Books.

Hawkes, J. W. (2006). *Cell-level healing: The bridge from soul to cell*. New York, NY: Atria Paperback.

Herman, J. L. (1992). *Trauma and recovery: The aftermath of violence – from domestic abuse to political terror*. New York, NY: Basic Books.

Hunt, V. V. (1989). *Infinite mind: Science of the human vibrations of consciousness*. Malibu, CA: Malibu Publishing Co.

Judith, A. (2004). *Eastern body, western mind: Psychology and the chakra system as a path to the self* (rev.). Berkeley, CA: Celestial Arts.

Kabat-Zinn, J. (1990). *Full catastrophe living: Using the wisdom of your body and mind to face stress, pain, and illness*. New York, NY: Bantam Dell.

Kabat-Zinn, J. (1994). *Wherever you go there you are: Mindfulness meditation in everyday life*. New York, NY: Hyperion.

Katie, B., & Mitchell, S. (2007). *A thousand names for joy: Living in harmony with the way things are*. New York, NY: Harmony Books.

King, S. (1981). *Imagineering for health: Self-healing through the use of the mind*. Wheaton, IL: Quest Books.

Kornfield, J. (2008). *The wise heart: A guide to the universal teachings of Buddhist psychology.* New York, NY: Bantam Books.

Kornfield, J. (2011). *Bringing home the dharma: Awakening right where you are.* Boston, MA: Shambhala Publications, Inc.

Lesser, E. (1999). *The new American spirituality: A seeker's guide.* New York, NY: Random House, Inc.

Levine, S. (1987). *Healing into life and death.* New York, NY: Anchor Books.

Levine, S. (1991). *Guided meditations, explorations and healings.* New York, NY: Anchor Books.

Levine, S. (2005). *Unattended sorrow: Recovering from loss and reviving the heart.* Emmaus, PA: Rodale Books.

Lübeck, W., Petter, F. A., & Rand, W. L. (2001). *The spirit of Reiki: The complete handbook of the Reiki system.* Twin Lakes, WI: Lotus Press.

Motz, J. (1998). *Hands of life.* New York, NY: Bantam Books.

Myss, C. (1996). *Anatomy of the spirit: The seven stages of power and healing.* New York, NY: Three Rivers Press.

Neff, K. (2011). *Self-compassion: Stop beating yourself up and leave insecurity behind.* New York, NY: HarperCollins Publishers, Inc.

Pert, C. (2004). *Your body is your subconscious mind* [CD]. Boulder, CO: Sounds True, Incorporated.

Petter, F. A., Yamaguchi, T., & Hayashi, C. (2003). *The Hayashi Reiki manual.* Twin Lakes, WI: Lotus Press.

Rand, W. L. (1998). *Reiki: The healing touch, first and sec-*

ond degree manual (rev.). Southfield, MI: Vision Publications.

Rand, W. L. (2003). *Reiki master manual.* Southfield, MI:
Vision Publications.

Rubenfeld, I. (2000). *The listening hand: Self-healing
through the Rubenfeld Synergy Method of talk and touch.*
New York, NY: Bantam Books.

Shainberg, D. (2000). *Chasing elephants: Healing psycho-
logically with Buddhist wisdom.* New York, NY: Asti-
Rahman Books.

Smith, E. W. L., Clance, P. R., & Imes, S. (Eds.). (1998).
Touch in psychotherapy: Theory, research, and practice.
New York, NY: Guilford Press.

Stevens, J. O. (2007). *Awareness.* Gouldsboro, ME: The
Gestalt Journal Press, Inc.

Sui, C. K. (1990). *Pranic healing.* York Beach, ME: Red
Wheel/Weiser.

Sui, C. K. (2000). *Pranic psychotherapy* (2nd ed.). Manila,
Philippines: Institute for Inner Studies Publishing
Foundation, Inc.

Thondup, T. (1996). *The healing power of mind: Simple
meditation exercises for health, well-being, and enlight-
enment.* Boston, MA: Shambhala Publications, Inc.

Thondup, T. (2000). *Boundless healing: Meditation exercises to enlighten the mind and heal the body.* Boston,
MA: Shambhala Publications, Inc.

Tolle, E. (1999). *The power of now: A guide to spiritual en-
lightenment.* Novato, CA: New World Library.

Tolle, E. (2005). *A new earth: Awakening to your life's pur-*

pose. New York, NY: Plume Books.

Usui, M., & Petter, F. A. (1999). *The original Reiki handbook of Dr. Mikao Usui.* Twin Lakes, WI: Lotus Press.

Weston, W. (1998). *Healing yourself.* Charlottesville, VA: Hampton Roads Publishing Company, Inc.

Yamaguchi, T. (2007). *Light on the origins of Reiki: A handbook for practicing the original Reiki of Usui and Hayashi.* Twin Lakes, WI: Lotus Press.

About the Author

Richard R. Curtin, Jr., Psy.D., RMT, is a licensed psychologist and Reiki Master Teacher. He has been practicing psychotherapy since 1975 and has received training in family systems therapy, addictions, trauma recovery, and cognitive behavior therapy. He began his Reiki training in 1994 and has been using Reiki in his psychotherapy practice since 1995.

Dr. Curtin teaches Reiki classes in the Usui method, Levels One, Two and Three, and Karuna Reiki™ in Cambridge and has also taught Reiki in the Continuing Education Program at the Massachusetts School of Professional Psychology in Boston. He is a member of the American Psychological Association, the Massachusetts Psychological Association, and the International Association of Reiki Professionals. He sees individual clients and couples, and runs training and supervision groups for psychotherapists and bodyworkers who are interested in using Psychotherapeutic Reiki. Please visit his websites at *www.cambridgecenterforchange.com* and *psychoterapeuti-creiki.com* for more information.

Made in United States
Orlando, FL
19 July 2023

35259295R10150